Praise for Bruce Northam's
In Search of Adventure: A Wild Travel Anthology

" . . . Pops the top off objective travel writing . . . Lives up to the adage that travel writers fear boredom more than death."

— *Time International*

" . . . 100 pithy travel stories . . . tales that are smart, funny and even risqué." — *National Geographic Traveler*

"This collection of travel tales doesn't just push the envelope, it shreds it."
— *San Francisco Examiner*

" . . . A collection of extraordinary memories, memories that conjure our own most moving journeys and make us hunger for more."

— *Salon*

"Body and soul are individually served." — *Publishers Weekly*

" . . . an engrossing read. And, for anyone who has ever dreamed of escape or imagined a wilder existence, this refreshing and sometimes over-the-top compilation will not disappoint." — *Newsweek.com*

" . . . the wanderlust-addicted writers of these exciting travel essays undergo physical challenges and life-changing insights as they explore seldom-visited places . . . zany, enthusiastic adventurers and hippie journalists push travel writing far beyond Sunday supplement fare."

— *Boston Herald*

"Anything can happen when you travel. And in the new anthology . . . just about everything does . . . dozens of writers share 100 amazing tales and take you to places you might never go. The book celebrates the wild side of travel." — *New York Post*

"Roughing It: The rough-and-ready contributors would probably eat their luggage before they'd pack a velvet tea gown or shooting tweeds. If they have luggage at all — this is the crowd that travels with a toothbrush, a pair of jeans, and a passport. They're an eclectic crew of adventurers..."   — *Washington Post*

"...be entertained, enlightened, and sometimes shocked by these honest slices of life on the road."   — *Travel Weekly*

"Lovers of storytelling and anyone looking for summer vacation inspiration shouldn't miss this."   — *San Francisco Bay Guardian*

"The anthology is a fresh, irreverent look at international travel, and delves into areas often glossed over, including experiences with crime, sex, and religious fraud."   — *San Francisco Chronicle*

Praise for Bruce Northam's *The Frugal Globetrotter*

"...there's no shortage of travel books on the shelves, but most aren't worth your time. We found (one) worth recommending: *The Frugal Globetrotter.*"   — *Men's Health*

"For more cheap travel ideas, read *The Frugal Globetrotter.*"
     — *Mademoiselle*

"...an offbeat look at saving while seeing...delving into subjects such as endangered paradises and women traveling alone...lots of practical advice."   — *Boston Globe*

Praise for Bruce Northam's multimedia lectures

"Insightful . . . Excellent program . . . adventures that are available to everyone with an open mind . . . highly recommend [his] program to other campus organizations." — North Carolina State University

"Bruce Northam rocks! . . . This guy is exciting, fun, and full of enough information to get anyone interested in truly enjoying life . . . shows us that we're only confined to the extent that we limit our dreams . . . This guy needs to hit every college campus in the nation." — University of Tulsa

"Ingenious methods to grasp hold of an enormous range of traveling opportunities . . . well-organized, entertaining and vibrantly clear, offering information that immediately elicited a positive response. . . . an intriguing and valuable guest speaker at any institution."
— University of Virginia

"It was obvious that his presentation was enjoyed . . . informative and funny and very knowledgeable." — Oklahoma State University

"Lecture was both fun and informative . . . everyone who went thoroughly enjoyed it. You inspired a lot of people to go out and explore the world as you have done." — University of the Pacific

"Wonderful presentation . . . people around here are still talking about it."
— Rutgers University

"Envious of your energy and enthusiasm. The students appreciated your vitality, but particularly responded to your varied interests evidenced by your travel experiences and your practical advice. In your presentations there is wit, humor, and a sly commentary on life."
— Lynchburg College

Globetrotter Dogma

ALSO BY THE AUTHOR

In Search of Adventure: A Wild Travel Anthology

The Frugal Globetrotter

100 canons for escaping the rat race

globetrotter dogma

& exploring the world

Bruce Northam

New World Library
Novato, California

New World Library
14 Pamaron Way
Novato, California 94949

Cover design and illustration: Mary Beth Salmon
Text design and layout: Mary Ann Casler
Interior illustrations: Denise Gardner

Library of Congress Cataloging-in-Publication Data

Northam, Bruce —. (Bruce Thoreau)
Globetrotter dogma : 100 canons for escaping the rat race and
exploring the world / Bruce Northam.
p.   cm.
ISBN 1-57731-216-3 (pbk. : alk. paper)
1. Travel. 2. Travel—Anecdotes.
3. Northam, Bruce (Bruce Thoreau)
I. Title.

G151 .N673 2002
910.4—dc21   2002000739

First printing, April 2002
ISBN 1-57731-216-3
Printed in Canada on acid-free, partially recycled paper
Distributed to the trade by Publishers Group West

10 9 8 7 6 5 4 3

To my parents,
Basil and Johanna, to whom I owe so much

CONTENTS

PROLOGUE

Not a shred of evidence exists that wandering is irresponsible. One trip can change everything, and every trip should try.

Attack boredom. Boredom is the fiery assassin. Sadly, modern humankind has become a prisoner of time and technology. We've been seduced into abandoning our innermost nomadic callings. The art of traveling is ancient, like cave art. A fresh nomad steps onto a globe that's been spinning for an unfathomable cycle of generations before he or she even opts to make the move.

When it comes to choosing to stay or go, you've got to know who's talking — your heart, your mind, or perhaps your DNA. You don't need to know what your predecessors found while wandering about — but you wonder, what were they looking for, and what did they find? Hints and cues have been passed down, from generation to generation, to the people you will meet traveling. You can't learn it *all,* but go meet them — and dare mighty things. Today is a gift.

Our wisdom tends to be a bit older than we are. In the mid-1800s, Henry David Thoreau suggested, "He who is only a traveller learns things at second-hand and by the halves, and is poor authority." Point taken, Mr. Thoreau — guilty as charged. But in a modern sense, I beg to differ. Here and now, the third millennium's information overload has rendered us half authority on far too much of what is real. Our computers have memories, but no remembrances.

The traveler, in turn, revives firsthand human discovery. These moments don't always find you; now and then you must find them. You must *go there* to find the beauty that makes other parts of the earth lonely.

INTRODUCTION

The adventure begins when the plan fails. Blurry plans provoke adventure, blind plans crash into it.

Do we spend the first half of our lives figuring out what we want to do with the second half of our lives, or do we spend the second half of our lives wondering what the heck happened in the first half? It's a tough call. And traveling helps us decide.

After circling the globe a few times, freestyle, I wrote *The Frugal Globetrotter* and *In Search of Adventure*. These books inspire my multimedia presentations to colleges and universities about what I've observed and learned *out there*. The canons of wandering contained in this book aren't rules of the road, just random road-tested musings — globetrotter lore to simply remind and inspire you to hit the road and enrich your journey. Dismiss common sense. Leave the herd for a while.

Globetrotter Dogma is a departure from my earlier travel writing. *The Frugal Globetrotter* supplied the nuts, bolts, will, and the *why* needed to quit your job and circle the globe for a year. *In Search of Adventure* anthologized assorted travel tales. This book is more like a timeless conversation, an ode to freestyle wandering — "rat-race exit blueprints."

This book was born when I transcribed the freedom rantings I communicate from university stages across America.

These aphorisms on travel eventually found their way into *Blue Magazine* and onto my literary agent's desk.

I also wrote this book because every now and then we all need a lift. The world is a much safer place than it appears in the media. Like a Disney movie, there is always one evil character messing with the plot, but that's *not* reality. While exploring the planet it becomes obvious that, for the most part, we live in a self-policing world. People take care of each other. Good neutralizes the bad. It's embedded in human nature. The *sour apples* can't compete with the sweet ones, so here are one hundred reasons to continue exploring and embracing our evolving world.

Get out of line. There is no time for a deadly outbreak of reserve.

"You ain't seen nothing yet."
> — Cab driver's response to a tourist
> inquiry about the inscription
> "The Past Is Prologue" looming
> over the National Archives Building

"Let them try to take away what we have danced."
> — Gypsy maxim

HOW TO USE THIS BOOK:

We all get stuck in ruts and words can inspire us to get out of them. Vocabulary can be culturally specific. Our word-stock is molded by our environment — and vice versa. Take this book to your office — or whatever location currently confines you — and share it with someone. These musings will invite you and your friends to remold your environment even when you're stationary. Reinvent your place and simply refuse to have a bad time.

And, every individual has to find his or her own style. Unconsciously, we adopt patterns of speech, dress, and behavior that make us feel comfortable. We add to and alter these styles in the course of a lifetime. It's time to put on those travelin' shoes.

Go set your gypsy blood on fire.

Globetrotter Dogma

CANON 1: Motion creates emotion.

The roaming gene should not become out-selected over time. Walking never disappoints; it's a whimsical celebration of *right now.* My father and I walk together a lot. We undertook a two-hundred-mile trek across Wales, coast-to-coast, along Offa's Dyke — the grand earthwork project conceived in the eighth century by King Offa to separate England from Wales.

En route we befriended Holly, a Welsh woman who was clearly oblivious to stress's beck and call. We joined her for fifteen miles atop the long, curving ridge boundary of Brecon Beacons National Park. At dusk the three of us spotted an elderly lady and her beagle hiking toward us. Teetering along on a walking stick, she wore a motoring cap and clutched a bunch of wildflowers. I said hello and asked her where she was going. She replied in Welsh, *"Rydw i yma yn barod."* We looked to Holly for a translation.

"She said, 'I'm already there, I'm already there.' "

They continued their placid conversation in Welsh until the old woman moved on. As she faded into the distance, I declared my envy for her philosophy. "Let's catch up with her," I said. "There's something else I'd like to ask." We spun around and caught up with her. She walked a few more steps along the trail, traded her flowers into the other hand, and raised an eyebrow. We scrutinized each other for a moment, beings from different eras and opposite sides of an ocean. I marveled at her vibrancy; she contemplated our shift in direction.

Holly translated my question, "What's the secret to a long and happy life?"

She directed her answer to Holly. "Moments."

There was a quiet pause. Then the old woman smiled, squinted at my father, and spoke slowly, "Moments . . . moments are all we get. A true walker understands this."

Moments. Yes. A year before this trek, I got the news that my father was seriously ill. A long moment, that. No more walks, no more calls, no more . . . moments. No more golden sunsets concluding a day of long-distance hiking. Well, he was seventy. But a moment is all it takes to change your direction, take a single step, then another. Soon the distance is met. My dad endured an open-heart bypass and back surgery. Miraculously, one year later we're savoring Celtic wisdom.

After a silent, timeless minute, we all clutched hands with the old woman, hugged, and waved good-bye. Just before she faded into the horizon, I looked back at her, plodding on with eternal poise and bearing. I sent a smile to my father. She's right — that is all we get.

"Try to keep your mind as open as the road, and good things are sure to follow."   — Jorma Kaukonen

CANON 2: Even if you are on the right track, you'll get run over if you just sit there.

I rode a sluggish train across humid southwest India that chugged slowly enough to keep inside the cloud of its own dust. Stopped in a nameless station, I tuned into a canine emissary. From my window I saw a dog, which, gristly and blue, sat before the open window of the seat adjacent to mine, where it knew a couple was eating. The gaunt dog had lost patches of fur, giving him the topography of a plucked chicken. I noted it was a he. He had a clever, longing face with eyes that radiantly reflected his thoughts: hunger, optimism, and patience, with a weary intuition of impending disappointment.

The couple next to the adjacent window had rotund physiques. Chewing blindly, stuffing themselves, they sensed no obligation to the dog, who continued eyeing them, sitting sidesaddle on his haunches. There was another dog further up the platform, to which an elderly man had thrown a tidbit. My dog glanced sideways for an instant, wondering whether to abandon his pitch — the couple might relent at any moment, since they had ample rations. Thought spread across his face, nostrils flared with the scent of bread and meat. He opted to stay put, his eyes infused with such yearning that I was sure the couple could no longer ignore him; they would look down and pitch at least a crust. But they didn't look away from their meal. Abruptly, the whistle sounded and the train started rolling. The dog cantered along with it half-heartedly, eventually graduating into a loping gallop.

Out of sight, past the station platform, I stuck my head out the window and saw the dog trot back to reclaim his spot on the platform and wait for the next train.

Hope: a commentary on the past and a promise for the future.

"Hope deferred maketh the heart sick."

— Proverbs 13:12

"My past and my present are sparring."

— Girlfriend explaining indecision

CANON 3: Give your jaw a break. Endure the sacred silence. Try abandoning words.

While on a long bicycle journey to *wherever,* I happened on a lone Chinese woman tending a crop in a barren, rolling field. I dismounted my bike as she leaned her chin on the handle of her shovel. Mutually surprised by the encounter, we scrutinized each other for a moment. We were two people who couldn't have come from farther corners of the earth. I

wondered how she kept her white dress spot-less working in the fields, while she puzzled over why I might be riding a bicycle through her quarter. After a silent, timeless minute, we simultaneously burst into smiles. Feeling self-conscious yet lighthearted, we  continued smiling at each other for what seemed like eternity. Then I waved a good-bye and rode away. Before coasting out of view behind a hilltop, I glanced back at her. There she stood, still leaning on her shovel, beaming and waving.

With her, I shared one of those inestimable aesthetic flashes: Silence is sometimes the best answer, even to an unasked question.

"When one jumps over the edge, one is bound to land somewhere." — D.H. Lawrence

CANON 4: You won't behold the sea until you turn your back on the shore.

I'm sitting in a kayak in a hidden cove somewhere in the Mergui Archipelago off the Andaman coast of Burma (Myanmar). Since time immemorial, Mergui waters, along with the west coast shores of Thailand and Malaysia, have been home to sea gypsies, floating nomad families living on ancient-design roofed boats made from big hollowed-out trees. Moken live-aboard vessel construction uses canoelike carved hulls, wood and bamboo pegs, rattan rope, and thatched palm leaves for roofs and sails. Kabangs resemble mini Noah's arks. The ingenious outriggers with mounted roofs are balanced and light for their twenty- to forty-foot-long stature and endowed to safely carry a family of up to eight through vicious Indian Ocean storms. No longer at their habitual moorings, they are instead fleeing from ethnic cleansing, dynamite fishing, land resettlement, "education," and this kayaker.

Moken philosophy focuses on pride in the face of scarcity. Kabangs symbolize the ownership of nothing — a formalized "letting go" — that uses identical scroll designs on the bow and stern to illustrate the digestion mouth-to-exit process that holds onto nothing permanently. This sapient design also announced to pirates through the centuries, "We have nothing to steal."

When a couple gets married, the community builds the newlyweds a boat, wherein they can start their own family. Children play either on or swimming around the boats. Women cook over an on-board fire, even when moored near a beach.

Monsoons direct the lives of this self-determining people. My friend and I paddle up next to a few families of Moken sea

gypsies musing in their dugout canoes. Sitting with paddles across their knees, they wait for the tide to go out. It has taken us days to find these elusive people who are born, live, and die at sea. On land, when we approached them, the invitation to exchange confidences evaporated, but approaching in a kayak seemed to lend a bit of credibility.

A Moken woman sat by herself in a small boat, an impossibly beautiful princess. The shy younger children's smiles could turn a barren landscape green. They don't speak any mainland language, but one elderly man knew some Burmese. Our Burmese guide directed my question to the princess, whose answers were then translated. "How is the fishing?" "Fish scared away — now over there," nodded the princess, paddling away.

I turned to my friend to jest about their sea-bound life being one way to avoid paying rent. This was unintentionally translated to the Moken family. The grandfather glanced our way, wincing at us with gentle, searching eyes, and spoke. The guide said something lost or found in translation, "Don't rent space in your head to just anyone."

The Moken are slowly dwindling as the world changes around them. But for as long as they last, they seem to be sublimely indifferent to all the despair going on in their country. The family floated away, enduring another military regime. The teenager turned around and lent one more Moken smile.

"All art, all education, can be merely a supplement to nature."
— Aristotle

"The fewer our wants, the nearer we resemble the gods."
— Socrates

CANON 5: More hugging, less mugging.

People are people; the rest is politics. In my travels I observed the number of times that people — conversing in parks, on street corners, and over restaurant meals around the world — touched each other per hour. Here's the deduction:

São Paulo, Brazil: 165
Paris, France: 80
Betong, Thailand: 19
Budapest, Hungary: 6
Tampa, Florida: 3
Reykjavík, Iceland: 1
London, England: 0

Hmmm.

Don't be afraid to reach out and touch someone. Tactile people are innately more at ease in mixed company. Sometimes a good hug is all you need. Doubtless the borders around sexuality are more porous today, but a hearty

embrace need not be reserved only for lovers, siblings, and friends. Fun is free.

A note of caution: Be sure you understand the local customs regarding physical affection before executing this canon.

"New earths, new themes, expect us."
— Henry David Thoreau

CANON 6: You'll never know what's on the other side until you land there.

In Irian Jaya, I assumed the identity of Frisbee Lord. But first a question: What is it about modern culture that it feels the need to impose a foreign language, way of life, and religion on a people that sit semi-nude and smiling, living in communion deep in an impenetrable forest? The well-intended but genocidal policies of outsiders continue as eastern Indonesia's West Papuan highland tribes succumb to alien coercion. One force driving this aborigine extermination is frontier psychology. Sledding to the Poles, summiting

11

Everest, rowing across the Atlantic Ocean — it's *all* been done. However, in an age when earthbound pioneer glory is virtually unattainable, I partook in a premiere — playing naked Frisbee with Stone Age–style equatorial West Papuan natives. Someone had to do it.

The black Melanesian aborigines still wear only penis gourds, an early-model jockstrap made from petrified yellow squash shells fitted over the genitalia and fastened skyward by thin strings tied around the waist. Wearing one is akin to sporting only a small, curved wiffleball-bat sheath. The women wear only skimpy grass skirts. Even today, representatives of these tribes unknown to the outside world periodically emerge from the forests. In 1990, a previously unidentified group surfaced. Ambassadors of the tribe, evidently shocked by what they saw, immediately disappeared again.

But they really took a shine to Frisbee. They were riveted by this simple aircraft, which employs the basic principles of physics. The flying saucer captured their imagination and made them belly-laugh. Initially, I was concerned that by introducing this game, I was further adding to the ruination of a traditional way of life that deserved to be preserved. But Western influence is on the rise and no doubt there to stay. A Frisbee is harmless, and they really enjoyed hurling it. Unanimous happiness cemented the verdict. And it isn't difficult for them to replicate a disc using preexisting items — their rattan "place mats," we discovered, also flew.

While other tradition-defying forces impose religion and outlander values, I tossed in my Sputnik. Upon entering a small village, I'd stroll into an open area, usually the courtyard in the midst of the *honay* complex, and spin the disc so it hovered and descended gradually into the waiting huddle. Some ran to it, some ran from it and kept on running. It was perhaps the biggest single event to hit these villages since the first explorer donated matches. Now *that's* ultimate Frisbee. The West Papuan natives, having developed for millennia in isolation, have many unique traits, including a hunting talent for throwing and launching spears. Straightaway, many of the younger flying disc converts advanced from having never seen a disc to being able to wing it fifty yards — using unconventional hand techniques.

I played sort of nude, too. At first, my gourd was uncomfortable; some of us wage a continuing struggle against fashion. The string tied around my waist failed to hold up the hardened vegetable-skin case that kept fumbling downward, and it itched. I didn't like sprinting barefoot across rocky fields, and I was paranoid about injuring my scrotum. I concluded that some of them intentionally tossed the Frisbee astray so I'd have to run for it. They laughed at that too.

It will be some time before Frisbees rival the importance of pigs in this quiet corner of the world where pigs are central to a family's economic and social status. Near the end of my sojourn back in time, I entered a village and tossed the flying disc into another curious horde. The village chief had difficulty catching, throwing, and comprehending it, as did some of the other elders. His discontent with the game grew when the disobedient aircraft drifted into the pigpen, spooking the priceless swine. The chief abruptly disappeared into the men's *honay*.

The sun was setting and the Frisbee fanfare winding down when the chief reappeared. Strutting erect, bows and arrows slung across his back, he paused in the center of the village and drew an arrow. Focusing, he aimed skyward at the hovering disc. A second later the Frisbee's heart was punctured. Crippled, it wobbled to earth. Justice. My realometer flared. The chief retrieved the impaled UFO and retired into his hut. Game over.

The wind whistled through my gourd.

"Why is it that humans created themselves a world into which they no longer fit biologically?"

— Sociologist David Woods,
beholding a heap of trash in the wilderness

CANON 7: The first thing you pack is yourself.

. . . and *that* should be an open, positive-thinking, compassionate person. Pack to give away: clothes, footwear, bungee cords, safety pins, and other convenience items we take for granted. Someone you meet may need them more than you do. Airline give-away paraphernalia (slippers, eyeshades, toothbrushes) make great gifts, especially in undeveloped countries. Business-class travelers always leave these gifts behind, so collect them as you deplane. Kids love balloons. People who've never seen an ocean are enthralled by seashells. Photos of friends and family also create a buzz. Pack a favorite music mix or two — lost Brazilian villages sometimes have generators that produce a few hours of juice a day. Many people learn English via music.

Protect your ears. Along with safeguarding snore-stressed marriages, earplugs are protection against blaring buses, trains, and obnoxious human beings.

Choose guidebooks that will support your mission — whatever it may be. Experiment by comparing what several different guidebooks say about a locale with which you are already familiar.

Think about your backpack. Before stuffing it, recognize that the real essentials

15

are what's in a globetrotter's head — background knowledge, resourcefulness, and sensitivity. A vital commodity to bring on any trip is an open mind. Usually, *people* make a place.

"The most important feature of a backpack is dah zippers [pronounced zipiz] When zippers fail, a backpack it ain't. Darker colors hide dirt. Thieves, like bugs, are lured to bright colors."   — JFK airport baggage handler

CANON 8: Truly leave home *home.*

A decade of international travel without email made me. Unwired, it's easier to discover who you are and what you stand for. When you detach, absolutely leaving home at its geographical point, the task at hand becomes living in the present.

There is some irresponsibility attached to avoiding new communication technology and cutting yourself off from possibly vital information about loved ones. But when email stormed into our everyday 1990s existence and cybercafés sprouted worldwide, many en-route travelers gradually segued from *gone* to still connected. This took the necessity out of starting over socially and eliminated the old-fashioned rendezvous tricks like swearing by guest house message boards,

meeting on a certain date in the last bar listed in the yellow pages, or in the café nearest the post office.

Remember, home is where the payments are.

"It is easier to suppress the first desire than to satisfy all that follow it." — Benjamin Franklin

"This no place like home."

— Cypriot Night Club bouncer
explaining local hospitality laws

"Many a man who thinks to found a home discovers that he has merely opened a tavern for his friends."

— George Norman Douglas

CANON 9: Dance.

Economic prudence once led me to a Caracas, Venezuela, dance hall where the languid human scenery relaxed with a steady balm-climate *mañana* attitude. Usually, the higher up on the socioeconomic ladder one travels, the more the likelihood of meeting an English-speaking acquaintance increases. In easygoing local joints on the "wrong side of town" your chances of encountering an *amigo* capable of speaking

English are slim. No worry; lacking Spanish skills makes your search for a dance partner a bona-fide challenge.

One option is to persuade one of the more experienced *señors* or *señoritas* to familiarize you with the hand and foot placements. Another is to watch other couples' hands and feet out of the corner of your eye until you get the hang of it. Even the language-impaired visitor soon realizes that dancing, like eating, is routine here, a national pastime, where everyone's clued in. Albeit alive and deliberate, dancing faces remain expressionless, as dreamy eyes hover calmly aloft dimly lit, slyly meshing torsos. Try to treasure the sundry close-up dances and the immediate, innocent intimacy. Dancing to Venezuelans is as normal as eating, unlike in the States, where people are typically either self-conscious or ego-driven loons.

Dancing endures as a hedonistic life force that's neither deadly nor illegal. Wherever you roam, discover local music scenes by hanging around the "tape market." Locate the freelance outdoor cassette and CD stalls, and when you hear something that moves you, find out where the musicians are performing. Dance zones are indifferent to status, and infectious music lets UBU.

"For wayfarers of all times, the right strategy for skillfully spreading the way essentially lies in adapting to communicate. Those who do not know how to adapt stick to the letter and cling to doctrines, get stuck on forms and mired in sentiments — none of them succeed in strategic adaptation."

— Zhantang

CANON 10: Check out this world before the next.

This isn't a rehearsal. Travel is one human being meeting another, face-to-face, person-to-person, not tourist-to-native. Go where the local people have not yet grasped the tourist concept.

Remember, we are all one. Find out for yourself what a miraculous world we live in, contrary to media portrayals. Realize that, sane or loony, we are all here together, and like it or not, this is it. Boost your mental, physical, and spiritual well-being — take a recess from the nine-to-five habit and chart your own authentic, unrefined, outward-bound escapade.

If you found out that you had one year left to live, what would be your most important goals in that last year? If traveling surfaces as one of them, why wait? Take a time-out, attend the global university, and get your Ph.D. in results. I only offer the travel wand; you are the magician that can wield it.

As the global village shrinks, we become increasingly aware of our interdependence. Because we all play a part, however small, in the interlocking of cultures, our new objectives should include having firsthand interactions with the staggering beauty and diversity of our planet.

I have got my leave. Bid me farewell my friends!
I bow to you all and take my departure.
Here I give back the keys of my door — and give
up all claims to my house.
I only ask for last kind words from you.
We were neighbors for long,
but I received more than I could give.
Now the day has dawned and the lamp that lit my
dark corner is out.
A summons has come and I am ready for my
journey.

— Indian poet-philosopher Rabindranath Tagore

"The world is a beautiful book, but of little use to him who cannot read it."   — Carlo Goldoni

CANON 11: Go where the locals go.

Cops and bartenders know their terrain better than the local chamber of commerce — and they work nights. Cordially interview them when you roll into town. Inquire about the best meal deals, zones of peril, inviting accommodations, safe strolling, camping, worthwhile attractions, and colorful hangouts.

"Better an honest loincloth than a fancy cloak."
— Swahili proverb

CANON 12: Go ahead and cry.

People misbehave when they're not feeling loved. I remember one evening on a Japanese subway when an angry drunk man was verbally abusing an elderly woman. Another passenger, trained in aikido, bristled and prepared to interfere. Just before violence broke out, an elderly man intervened: "Whatcha drinking?" he asked. "Whiskey," replied the ornery drunk. The elderly man said, "My wife died last year, she and I used to love to drink whiskey together." A conversation

21

ensued, and ten minutes later, the mean-spirited man sobbed, his head resting in the old man's lap while the old man stroked his head, giving him the consolation he needed.

✦ ✦ ✦

One lonely night in Malaysia, in the midst of a year abroad, I saw *Harry and the Hendersons,* a silly G-rated movie about a family who adopt a lovable Bigfoot. I sobbed and felt much better.

"And which part of the world is suffering in your absence, madam?"

— inquiry from a New Delhi rickshaw driver
to travel writer Pamela Michael

CANON 13: Make do.

Allegedly, our experiences are the mere darting of ions and swirling of neurochemicals, creating vivid first-person, present-tense subjective sensations of sound, color, despair, lust, and glee. But it's a little different when *you* dart and swirl.

I've run risky rivers in a mix of wooden, rubber, steel, and plastic inventions, but none caused more hyperventilation than

negotiating the Waiqa (pronounced *wine-gah*) River in a classic Fijian bamboo Bilibili raft, after a fat rain. If retrograde amnesia could be willfully activated, I'd enjoy it now.

Imagine balancing on a long floating ski and surfing that tippy bamboo toboggan through a whitewater maze flanked by unforgiving, vertical stone canyon walls. At first, the idea of rafting rapids on five twenty-five-foot bamboo trunks lashed together by twine seemed logical, like going bowling with an eggplant. Elected second in command of one of two rafts, I stepped onto the back end of our craft, the senior pilot manning the front end. At first I wasn't sure what to do with the ten-foot bamboo pole in my hand.

Two guys balancing precariously on opposite ends of something seemingly designed for a log-rolling contest. We (he) jockeyed this needle through a narrow aqua chasm with a bag of navigating tricks you don't learn in gym class. This energy is not identified with civilization but with the flight from it.

On the other boat, two barefoot men also hustled their two- by twenty-five-foot bamboo raft down what began as a wide, delta-winding river. The extremely tippy temperament of the watercraft was put to one test in the open water; the white-water raging gorge was another. The winding river suddenly entered a narrow gorge where parallel rock walls pinched the river into a rampaging froth. The sun stood noon-high between the walls, except when covered by canopy. Unsquint. We glided onward, gaining speed.

I used my guiding pole basically to bother fish. Up front the extreme-Venetian pilot maneuvered surpassingly well to keep my pack and camera upright — which sat, tied upright on the back of an African Queen seat in the center of the craft. The nearly interlocking walls of the gorge were storm-born architecture. Misty, wavy airborne spray.

Like when you're running the Grand Canyon, there is no turning back. People float on long bamboo rafts in other parts of the world; they don't navigate narrow-canyon white water in them. Rubber bounces off rock walls, bamboo splinters.

Their bewildering level of athleticism included using the guide poles to prevent collisions with suddenly appearing rocks and bending canyon walls, using a machete to slash overhead obstacles, and facing one another — in mid rapid — to casually clarify navigation. In times of peril, the lead men dove from the rafts — leaving me solo, nugatory — swam to shore, and then kept pace with the raft by sprinting barefoot along the riverbank over fallen trees and mossy boulders in order to dive in front of the boat and swim-kick-sway it away from unforgiving obstacles protruding just ahead. Highlanders begin undertaking this old trade route — formerly the primary access to sea level — at ten years old. Until recently, they had to walk back home.

Urgency flared when we encountered a massive palm tree that had fallen across the canyon, creating an unpassable dam. Though we were many foot miles from a road, the

logistical obstacle didn't faze the other three men at first. Then they exchanged a glance that said, "Nothing like this before."

Their emergency portage solution would impress even a knife juggler. Fretless, they separated to opposite banks. One took a machete swipe at the base of a forty-foot rubber tree, the high end falling next to the guy on the opposing bank. Upriver, holding the rafts close to a vine, I watched them *share* the machete — to cut long strips of bark — by hurling the hulky knife back and forth to each other across the raging thirty-foot-wide river. They casually hucked the glistening machete back and forth like playground pals tossing a tennis ball, systematically cutting enough peels of bark to bind one long piece of forest twine, used to guide the rafts over the tree.

I knew if their Fijian mojo held, we'd prevail.

We portaged around the obstacle and cruised on. The river continued swinging through the rock and the centuries. Droopy green gardens, waterfall drizzles, sunlight shimmering through mist, vines. Crashing rapids and high water fraught with sweet air.

The meander through the gorge walls diminished back to flat open water and plains of palms, where billowing bamboo trees once again dominated the landscape. Words fail. We pulled out at the confluence with the unhurried Monasavu River, enjoying a hearty lunch in a local home. True freedom, far from the planet's widening roads.

It takes one man two days to build a Bilibili. The long and

narrow boats built for the Waiqa Gorge journey are one-way crafts, left downriver for anyone heading seaward or needing wood for construction or firewood.

"Get on your knees and thank the Lord you're on your feet." — Irish toast

CANON 14: Think before you give.

We may not have strip-malled the entire planet yet, but everything we do has an impact. While trekking high in Nepal's Himalayas, ten days walk from electricity and political sex scandals, I happened on a medicine-chest-sized mirror hanging on a teahouse wall. In an action reminiscent of my juvenile epoch, I removed the mirror from the wall, walked outside, and used it to transmit the immensely powerful sun reflection around the village.

Fifty Nepalese villagers, led by a curious elderly woman, soon gathered to witness the miracle of this invention that had started to transmit the almighty solar laser beam to villages across the valley.

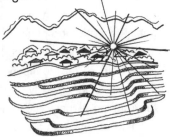

For the remainder of the day, as I gradually hiked up and away from the village, the elderly woman sun-beamed *me* every twenty minutes. Though they'd always had the means to flash, things may never be the same there.

Weeks later, back in Kathmandu, miscellaneous trekkers provided consistent reports about a small, arcane mountain village that emitted a mysterious twinkling that seemed to be directed at incoming hikers.

✦ ✦ ✦

The high-desert town of Creel looms over Mexico's green and wooded Copper Canyon. The Sierra Tarahumara Amerindians live in the canyons below. I ventured with a few comrades into an archetypal dive bar misnamed Club Superior. After a Spanglish discourse on North America's largest canyon system, I bought an inebriated narrator a beer. After chugging it, he parked the bottle on the bar, gazed into space, and tipped over backward off his stool.

"Excuse me sir, would you happen to have any Grey Poupon?"   — New York City panhandler

CANON 15: Take advantage of foot power.

Lose the main road. You don't always need a plan. Stay off the interstates; they hide landscapes and people.

Go up to the roof of the place you're staying. Once you can see, you can see. Look around and pick an interesting direction to go for an all-day walk. Bring a daypack with your camera, a notepad, and some water. Then just smile and be open to meeting new people. If you pass an interesting factory, school, or business, go in and check it out. In many places, particularly in underdeveloped countries, people are happy to let you watch their daily work, whether it's making hats, drying fish, or teaching math to a roomful of eight-year-olds. This is where fun hides.

The audience is equal to the piece of art.

"Throw some tea and bread in an old sack and jump over the back fence." — John Muir on expedition planning

Nature writer E.W. Teale noted that "Muir was rescued from the threat of financial success." While supervising a broom handle factory, he was working on a lathe belt when a file flew up and hit him in one eye, blinding it. In immediate sympathetic reaction the other eye also went blind. Muir lay in bed for three days taking no food or water and spent a total of

four weeks lying in a darkened room thinking he would never see again. When his sight returned he took a walk through the woods, seeing trees, wildflowers, and all that nature had to offer. Muir made a decision on the spot: He would never again make a living related to tools or machinery.

What to do? It was an easy choice for Muir: take a three-year sabbatical, including a thousand-mile walk from Indianapolis to Cedar Key, Florida, steering by compass, avoiding the cities, through forests, over mountains, swimming streams and rivers. At one point in the journey he came upon a solitary flower that brought tears to his eyes.

"I see more of what is going on around me because I am not concerned with finding a parking place."
— Taxi driver wisdom

CANON 16: Avoid the Unsavory Tourist Syndrome.

Six Americana impulses that shout *tourist!* as you bumble abroad are:

1. High-fiving everyone.
2. Wearing high-top sneakers and a baseball cap backward.

3. Talking incessantly, volume set on loud. Observation: There are *two* North American languages: English and louder.
4. Defending American football players against charges that they're overpadded, compared to helmetless, and possibly toothless, rugby players.
5. Giving an enthusiastic thumbs–up, accompanied by a lightheaded grin.
6. Prefixing your sentences with "yo" and "like." Responding with "totally" and "definitely!" Then high-fiving again.

"There are only two emotions in a plane: boredom and terror."
— Orson Welles

CANON 17: "Remember what you have seen, because everything forgotten returns to the circling winds." — lines from a Navajo wind chant

Wherever you wander, behold sunsets whenever possible. It's therapeutic to gaze into the sun as it sails into the horizon, allowing the lithium rays to nourish your genius. Sunsets are involuntarily the most pensive minutes of the day.

I saw a man pursuing the horizon;
Round and round they sped.
I was disturbed at this;
I accosted the man.
"It is futile," I said,
"You can never —"

"You lie," he cried,
And ran on.
                    — Stephen Crane

Surrendering to a sunset on a Costa Rican ocean-front lounge, the proprietor identified an osprey (fishing hawk) and a bare-throated tiger heron. The breezy sunset ritual was the ceremonial closing of another Central American day: rugged terrain excursions by day, simple elegance at night, a twilight moment of low-flying brown pelicans swooping across the reddening sky, inches above the water. Above the light thunder of nearby tide breaks, my associate nodded toward the flock of birds affirming, "There goes the Costa Rican Air Force." (Costa Rica has no military.) The scene was inescapably *tranquilo*.

"Things do not change; we change."
                    — Henry David Thoreau

globetrotter dogma

CANON 18: Bypass neurotic travel partners.

Sometimes it's a good idea to rove solo, since spending *all* of your time with anyone breeds dementia. Nine-to-fivers don't fully comprehend "twenty-four/seven" until they've crossed India on a bus with a travel partner. If you travel with someone, make sure you are able to separate periodically. In healthy relationships, our love for each other outshines our need for each other. (I'm not saying that love isn't grand.)

"As with anything enormously attractive, we are obsessed only with getting in; we can worry later about getting out."
— Edward Abbey

"Love stinks."
— J. Geils Band

CANON 19: Try solving the Marriage Puzzle.

The Jakun tribe inhabits a naturally wild jungle adjacent to peninsular Malaysia's Endau Rompin National Park. The surrounding south-central mountains rise northward up the center spine of this narrowest landmass of Southeast Asia into Thailand and Burma, eventually connecting with the Himalayas.

The animist Jakun have irrepressible smiles and an interesting tradition determining romantic connections. No complex codes govern courtship here. Instead they have a social-Darwinist Rubik's Cube of sorts. Their marriage puzzle is a pencil-sized section of bamboo that is snaked through by one continuous string loop to create two smaller, intertwined string loops. From each loop hangs a bamboo ring. In order to marry within the tribe you must be able to figure out how to move both rings to one loop.

Knee-wobbling charisma doesn't go very far in Jakun culture. A bit of tribal technology imposes the buffer between men and women.

With coaching from a villager, it took me ten minutes to figure out the puzzle. Another writer in his fifties was still twisting fruitless knots when we departed hours later. (Today, he remains a bachelor.)

"Wildebeests have been known to run themselves to death while attempting to elude mosquitoes."

— The bachelor who couldn't solve
the marriage puzzle, comparing human
divorce to the kill-or-be-killed realm of wild game

P.S. It was the accepted practice in Babylon four thousand years ago that for one month after a wedding the bride's father would supply his son-in-law with all the mead he could drink. Mead is a honey beer and because their calendar was lunar-based this period was called the honey month or what we know today as the honeymoon.

CANON 20: Let it rain.

Since the Second World War, trailblazer types have filtered in and out of Irian Jaya, Indonesia's remote highland valleys. Few others have had the fortune of befriending Ruuf, my *Dani* guide for the first leg of my trek. Calm, wise, and barefoot, he led me, leaping nimbly from slippery log to log.

When I lost him, I tracked his mud prints. A meshed *billum* bag made of long grass, slung around his forehead and draped across his back, contained sweet potatoes, a palm-leaf mat that doubled as a rain poncho (resembling a flight-worthy nun's habit), compressed tobacco, leaves for rolling cigarettes, and a small bag of salt. It was his primordial briefcase.

Unexpected downpours are common. One monsoon shower was especially enlightening. Betrayed by flooded boots and soaked by sweat inside my rain gear, I caught Ruuf smiling under his temporal teepee, not one drop of water on him or his petrified-squash penis gourd. Pausing there in the downpour, I contemplated my departure from the essential laws of human survival. He was Darwinian perfection and I was a mail-order misfit, a defeated poster child of Western survival gear. I was seduced into surrendering to my innermost nomadic calling; the contents of my backpack later trans-formed into gifts. Luxuries are often not only dispensable, but frequently hindrances.

"The edge is where you put it." — Paul McHugh

CANON 21: Buy things there.

Buying locally helps you blend in and promotes compassionate capitalism. With the exception of Frisbees, feminine products, and antibiotic ointments for ferociously itchy insect bites, jock itch, and stinging bungs, you can often buy basic items cheaper en route. (Japan and Scandinavia are exceptions to this decree.) Unless you're scheming to ice climb or practice naked yoga above the tree line, hold off on buying boot crampons.

Honor your gift-purchase impulse on the road. An eight-dollar Balinese woodcarving makes a bigger impression than another T-shirt. With considerate tact and a keen eye, you can unearth and purchase marvelous souvenirs that are not officially "for sale" — at a fair price. The story behind procuring travel souvenirs often outshines the actual artifact. And the odyssey of hauling it home usually inspires yet another tale. Here are some tips:

+ The best places to locate interesting gifts are usually workplaces: factories, fish markets, and home-based craft workshops. Look for handmade tools, hunting paraphernalia, and whatever you deem art.
+ Be sensitive to "cultural rape." Make sure economically stressed people, especially aboriginals, are

parting with possessions they can replace easily with your payment. Don't be swayed by politeness regarding an item they will really miss. Acquiring gems necessitates culture-sensitive compromise; bargain with the correct individual.

✦ Remember that sometimes packages shipped from abroad (did someone say Turkish carpet?) never make it home. The tactics for negotiating fragile or "oversized" souvenirs onto your homebound flights and through customs also demand diplomacy. Always declare souvenirs as gifts on customs forms.

My northern Thailand fish trap combines lobster-trap ingenuity and jungle art. It consists of one section of bamboo aggrandized into a conical shell that houses an internal DNA-like bamboo stick helix. I knew the trap, tied to the outside of my backpack while transiting Bangkok, was a winner when scores of elderly men accosted me, admiring the artwork that recalled their youth, not to mention the perplexed stares it earned on the subway ride home from JFK Airport.

Note: Thirty seven-foot hunting spears will not fit into a flight attendant's coat cabin. While I was toting those Irian Jayan highland hunting spears on Thirty-fourth Street, the common push-and-bump pedestrian anarchy parted and cleared a path to allow my uninterrupted passage.

"Whatcha got there?"

— Concerned New York City policeman
eyeing the seven-foot-long Irian Jayan
hunting spears in Penn Station

CANON 22: Expect setbacks.

The Chinese character for crisis signifies both breakdown and opportunity. Have a book, a conversation, or a drink handy for waiting out avalanche-blocked roads or for when the trekking permit office in Kathmandu invents another holiday. Every now and then you might have to grin and bear a tourist trap; for reasons not even science can wholly explain, the allure of Las Vegas is creeping across the globe.

Traveling isn't going where you want, it's wanting to be where you already are. If you find a path with no obstacles, it probably doesn't lead anywhere. Life is like photography: We use the negative to develop.

"Well, it's been a wonderful evening. Kind of a shame we spent it here."

— Traveler, saying good-bye to writer of speeding ticket

CANON 23: Stay open to thumb luck.

Consider thumb touring. People are proud of their home-lands, and hitching is a dandy way to identify with a region — especially rural ones. Thumb-tour anonymity breeds honesty and more free therapy. Enter a different mind-set every hour!

The Japanese are a trusting people, and hitching is not a problem in Japan. A truck driver once gave me a lift from Tokyo to Osaka, bought me vending-machine soup and lunch midway, and continually tried to illustrate the immensity of Mount Fuji. The only word we had in common was *Madonna*. Arriving in Osaka after midnight, I had difficulty explaining to him that I needed to find a very cheap place to sleep. The confusion continued until he drove me to the police station in search of an interpreter. After a momentary exchange with the police, he waved good-bye and walked back to his truck. A policeman then set folded blankets and a pillow on a cot inside one of the jail cells. He motioned me into the cell, returning with biscuits and a glass of juice. Smiling and nodding, he said, "Morning," exited, and closed the door.

A note of caution: Hitchhiking can be very dangerous.

Don't be afraid to refuse rides from suspicious-looking drivers. If you must hitchhike, try creating a sign for a destination that's in the opposite direction of your actual destination and display it while thumbing in the direction of your desired destination. When a concerned driver pulls over to correct your blooper, explain your tactic and request a lift.

Other sign options: Please, Harmless, Free Beer, Mountains, Hello, Mom, Trees. I've even heard tales from a guy who used a gangly monkey puppet to consistently lure rides worldwide.

"Don't panic."   — Douglas Adams

"You didn't look like you stunk, so I pulled over."
                                    — John Edward Pentaleri

CANON 24: Have your mid-life crisis now.

Put your career guilt on hold. Don't postpone travel happiness indefinitely. A life of excessive work can be dreadful. Escape while you can. Listen to your heart and ignore the boss grimacing about your forthcoming sabbatical. Take everything in moderation, including moderation itself.

To be a star
You must shine
Your own light,
Follow your own path,
And don't worry
About the darkness
For that is when stars
Shine brightest.
        — Copied from a guest house wall in Singapore

Don't be a myopic human *bee*ing, change the flag of your palace, and beware the Dopeler Effect: the tendency of stupid ideas to seem smarter when they come at you rapidly. Screw orthodoxy, and take a recess from the least common denominator.

"Do your thing and I will know you."
                            — Ralph Waldo Emerson

CANON 25: "If you come to a fork in the road, take it." — Yogi Berra

And when you choose a fork, remember John Muir, paramount naturalist, the definitive lone wolf. A brilliant, intense, cantankerous man, his handsome features obscured by a beard suited for bird nesting, Muir had a passion for Yosemite Valley, with which he was locked in a lifelong metaphysical embrace that made his human associations secondary, at best. He was famous for climbing a Douglas spruce high in the mountains in the midst of a riotous thunderstorm, where he swayed back and forth in the topmost branches, yowling with crazy delight.

Muir was compelled to hike in the forest while a violent gale blew down trees, "at the rate of one every two or three minutes." Suddenly seized with an urge to climb a wind-whipped tree, he chose the tallest spruce in his range and had no trouble scaling the hundred-foot giant. Reaching his perch near the top, he clung like "a bobolink on a reed." Pitching forward and backward in an arc of twenty to thirty degrees,

he reveled with the waves of wind bending vast regions of forested mountainsides, illuminated by a rainbow of shimmering light. He closed his eyes, listening to the rushing wind chaffing tree branches and savored

the piney fragrance streaming past. He clung to his perch for hours, exhilarated, only climbing down when the gale passed.

"Something utterly wild had crept into his nature."
— Loren Eisley, about John Muir

CANON 26: Europe can wait.

If you intend to behold the entire globe, visit the distant lands of undrinkable tap water and shamanism while your immune system is hearty. Save Western Europe for when negotiating stairs is a bitch.

And, believe me, when you do visit Europe don't try photographing the prostitutes in Amsterdam's red-light district unless you're wearing running shoes. After repeated rejection, I offered one pro the fee for her usual services to snap a photo. "Nope," she said, but I shot one anyway. Immediately an army of heel-clacking professionals were on the warpath, sprinting after me, intent on destroying more than my camera.

It can be difficult sometimes discerning where adventure stops and stupidity begins.

"Don't be such a cretin."
— Junior high school disciplinary principal

CANON 27: Know your boat.

Like a sailor, take care of your ship. Most boats sink not because of the way they were built, but because of the way they were maintained. Know your boat and respect its pace. The power boater is always trying to get there, and the sailor is always right where they want to be.

"Human responsibility will be shuffled through the computer, then no one is to blame. Computer responsibility versus human responsibility? Means people responsibility. Computer "misuse" can make lying a universal principle. Computers don't know how to go slow, and understand."
— Boatbuilder Brendan

"What is man without the beasts? If all beasts are gone, man would die from a great loneliness of spirit. For whatever happens to the beasts, soon happens to man. All things are connected." — Chief Seattle

"There are old pilots, and there are bold pilots. But there are no old, bold pilots."
— Words to fly by in the Alaskan bush

CANON 28: Experiment with the dome effect.

Get in touch with the urgent starscape by sleeping outside. At least once, exist outdoors for a week. Sleep on the roof. Snoozing under the stars puts you in touch with our celestial dome and inadvertently your own dome. Ponder that.

When it gets dark, the stars come out.

"In heaven an angel is nobody in particular."
— George Bernard Shaw

CANON 29: Consider inoculations.

There are two schools of thought about getting inoculations: absolutely and forget it. Many unvaccinated veteran travelers escape without incident, but some rookies get cerebral malaria. You decide. Your local or county health department should be cheaper than the tropical disease specialist, but they'll both send your itinerary to the Center for Disease

Control and probably urge the same thing — a bucketful of pills and shots. Avoiding many diseases, like malaria, is 90 percent prevention. Better safe than sorry. Try acupuncture and homoeopathy for what ails you both before you go as a preventative measure and if you get sick on the road. Many over-the-counter Western medical panaceas eventually backfire.

And there's no shot for food-borne diarrhea. If you think you've had a diarrhea nightmare don't appeal for sympathy from my cousin. He was so incapacitated in India by food poisoning that he was too weak to make it to a bathroom. He lay helpless under a palm tree, simultaneously exploding from both ends. Exacerbating the bad dream was having to physically ward off a family of insistent pigs vying for his outputs. Now there's an image for a Kaopectate ad.

"If you look like your passport photo, you're too ill to travel." — Will Kommen

CANON 30: Go to church.

The one I attended was a missionary-constructed Irian Jayan church, a racquetball court–sized wooden cabin with a corrugated tin roof, packed with quasi-clad worshipers. My view from the rear of the cabin was of women and young girls on the left, men and boys on the right. A lonely clock with a dead battery loomed above a makeshift wood-box altar — behind it stood the rambling missionary preacher, the only other person wearing clothes. Seated beside me was a man wearing only a beige gourd on his private part, a headband of greasy chicken feathers on his head, and a clove cigarette stored in his large earlobe pierce. Patiently waiting to interact with the preacher, he inserted a quarter moon–shaped pig bone into his pierced nasal septum. When their discussion began, everyone else listened intently, the women sitting with their netlike *billum* bags slung around their heads, bulging with provisions and babies. An unsympathetic gatekeeper declined to let people leave before the service concluded.

During prayer, all eyes were closed and heads lowered. The natives cover both eyes with one hand during prayers in fear of going blind. First came the peekaboo glances at the peculiar white man, then the restrained library chuckling. When the service ended the women rushed past me nervously to exit the church. The little girls were absolutely shocked by my presence. Then someone broke out a guitar and another ceremony emanated from the rear of the shrine, New Guinea style.

"We all travel the Milky Way together. When we try to pick out anything by itself, we find it hitched to everything else in the universe." — John Muir

"I am not an atheist but an earthiest." — Edward Abbey

CANON 31: Resist complaining.

Period. Complaining may be a symptom of failing to notice the beauty around you. If you must whimper, break out your translation dictionary or phrase book and transcribe your conundrum to a local. You may realize that your dilemma is a tad pathetic — and you might even learn the language.

After circling the western half of the Pacific Rim for a year, I hitchhiked, very gradually, from California to New York. Looking like unwashed trouble, I visited an illegal dump under a bridge outside Pittsburgh to look for material with which to make a destination sign.

I ran into some needy people collecting broken furniture (really, miscellaneous wood) to feed the barrel fire heating their ramshackle hideout. "Hunting wood, man?" one of them asked me.

"No, pal, I'm in cardboard," I answered, getting on my way.

"You can rest your head on my shoulder."
— Nicaraguan woman, who endured a torturously long bus ride, a ride I grumbled about, once a week.

CANON 32: Invent your own philosophy.

My ritualized dogma might inspire, but your wisdom belongs to you. Be skeptical of overarching and conflicting claims for salvation. We are all responsible for our own happiness.

Make your own rules. Appeal to your higher power and tune into your ideals, not the ones hurled at you by Madison Avenue.

Waiting on a curb at a Manhattan intersection, I observed a five-year-old boy whose mother restrained his attempt to cross the street despite the flashing "Don't walk" sign. The bridled son glanced up at his mother, added confusion to his expression, and clarified, "Yeah, but it doesn't say 'Don't Run.' "

"Catnip can affect lions and tigers as well as cats."
— Romanian donkey cart pilot, intimating
that "we're all in this together"

"Humble is a hard road to walk."
— One of the last speakers of the Nakota
language, standing on Moose Mountain medicine
wheel, Pheasant Rump Reservation, Canada

> *DIVIDE*
> *WISDOM*
> *Exit 102*

— sign, Interstate 15, Idaho

CANON 33: Accept culture shock.

Flashing into new habitats can rattle your mainframe. On your first time out surely you're going to get culture shocked. It's like a cold: You will get over it. Being stirred from jaded complacency forces us to notice.

The shocking images from around the world are the ones that stay with you. While visiting a hospital in Delhi, India, I observed a mother carrying her dead infant down a long dim hallway, out the front door of the hospital, and into her gruesomely impoverished neighborhood. Her face was like stone.

"What do you suppose will satisfy the soul, except to walk free?"
— Walt Whitman

CANON 34: Get lost, then keep going.

And when you get there, what do you do to overcome language barriers and break the ice in distant lands? Pantomime. Forsake some of your ingrained reality and be open to people who aren't racing on a hamster wheel. Get creative. Imitate animals: Trumpet like an elephant, caw like a raven, clap your feet and bark like a seal, and you'll have a connection (with the kids, at least). Humor lubricates the universe.

You can predict the length of your trip, but you must nurture the width and the depth of it.

The adventure begins when the pavement ends.

globetrotter dogma

"A pond without an inlet or an outlet stagnates."
— Brendan Lake

CANON 35: Your mind is the strongest
muscle in your body.

I'm jetting to Salt Lake City, throwing back pretzels, musing below at an endless desert. Hours later, I'm one of eight apprehensive fellows — in search of something not found anywhere near concrete — seated in a semicircle at the bottom of a southern Utah canyon, taking in a sunset lecture by a female outdoor survival guide on how to wipe your backside using a handful of fine red sand or sagebrush. Pine needles and sticks wound, she warns. This is prelude to a three-day fast that begins with an overnight speed hike through sandstone-cactus backcountry; we are relentlessly mobile, eating nothing, and drinking only the fishtanky water we find, frequently from puddles.

The fourteen-day field course is a canyon country wilderness four-stage marathon covering more than two hundred walking miles. It's an odyssey with missions — primitive wilderness living skills and a total detox from fast-paced advertising and Internet habitude. Out here, we elect to be forced into many situations as diverse as deep thought and

starving — which, I learn, go hand in hand. Hitherto, I took survival for granted

Hard learning follows hard lessons. Many were magnified in the wake of three days of extreme trekking without food. We set off at dusk, wearing only waist packs (minus water bottles), our belts dangling with tied-off garments, and one sparkly-blue enamel cup, suckling water from potholes that are also home to innumerable darting tadpoles. We set out for more Olympic walking through myriad terrain changes, the elevation rising and falling from ten thousand to five thousand feet. We're being pushed to simulate a survival situation. Jet-lagged and visiting from sea-level cement, I'm punchy with hungry exhaustion, reminding myself I can quit, but there's no refund. You can die, but there's that death waiver you signed.

En-route seminars include animal track identification (rear bear tracks look amazingly human), eating river birch leaves (tasting like . . . leaves), and the explanation for packing two pair of underwear: a backup for when you shit yourself from either nerves or lapping up buggy puddles. The gaze of angst widens.

We fall into routines of duct taping blistering toes and ergonomically stripping and tying off clothing onto our belts as the sun demands. The breakout sessions on knife use and making fire without matches are the "big leaps for humankind." We combust fire from carved sticks. We make bow drills by whittling a baseboard, a stringed stick-cum-bow, and spindle. Then imagine a mad pyro-fiddler spinning embers by wailing hurriedly back and forth with the bow on a handmade paper towel holder tipped on its side. The turning spindle point creates smoking friction with the baseboard. You plant the resulting ember into your fine-kindling bird's nest, blow, then appreciate matches for life.

Still no food. The mood swings from chatty to solemn. Guides are intentionally elusive about even the near future — they only act as safety nets in the event of an emergency. Five-minute breaks collapse into instant group naps.

As I was climbing out of canyon number ninety on day three, my supposedly high-tech mountain-fearless sneaker-boots herniate by flapping shoe-sole rubber like an eighteen-wheeler losing a retread. Branded into various zones on the sole are logos indicating the miraculous ability of each engineered area — intricate parts of footwear able to turn me into a wilderness machine. Soleless, I plod on, now wearing the equivalent of hospital slippers.

My contemplation on wearing slippers for the next eleven days is interrupted when the business school graduate and his associate become the Gatorade brothers by kneeling simultaneously to vomit lime-green antifreeze. Yakking up bile is normal under extreme exertion circumstances without food. The body expects scheduled snacks and secretes superfluous bile, causing nausea.

The sneakerboot blowout, however, was abnormal, so I duct tape my soles back on. In the midst of slicing tape sections to mummify my "boots," I glance away at the heaving-again Gatoradors and plant my knife a half-inch inside my thumb. Mommy flashes into my mind — nobody else notices her.

Duct taped in five regions, we march into another night. How much more can we take? By day four, you down a half-cup of oatmealish veggie mush, and you're bloated.

Workshops continue on flint napping, munching dandelion greens (the yellow part too), tying knots, setting animal traps, and expending fewer calories finding food than the caloric value of food found to endure in the outdoor super-market.

We're now handy at stone-grinding oats and barley into flour. The guide surmises that, "Consumers, never knowing where their food comes from, are out of touch with the circle of life." *Think* about your next burger.

One of our staples becomes sheep jerky, made by dangling strips of raw sheep meat on a rack baking in the sun. On a 1,500-calorie-per-day diet (rivaling a Snickers bar and fat stack of Pringles combo) it *all* tastes good, even the spongy texturized vegetable protein (TVP).

But the no-trail power walking ain't over. Our mobile homes are hand-tied backpacks made from military-issue ponchos wrapped around a wool blanket. Both are string bound like bakery cakes. The bundle is carried by one long section of seat-belt strap woven through the parcel and around both shoulders, then tied around your waist. We ration the supplies for the next five days: carrots, cornmeal, garlic, lentils, millet, potatoes, powdered milk, pepper, onion, salt, and vegetable bouillon — plus a cloth bag with enough peanuts and raisins to gorge a kitten.

Thinking our hard days are behind us, we realize it's time to sense this place. The aromas shift from juniper to armpit to sage to people battling digestive gas wars with the TVP. Living like a hunter-gatherer tribe shaved down to our humanity, we think the only apparent hazards are campfire smoke inhalation, being relaxed to the point of collapse, or getting a whiff of someone's breath (only baking soda is permitted to clean teeth).

At sunrise, no bother that my canteen of mossy agua was nearly frozen solid. I'm alone in a red canyon with two dilemmas:

1. While doing laundry naked by the river I sunburnt my butt cheeks. Must sleep on stomach, face down into ant ranch.
2. Once the stomach unbloats, an amazingly small amount of food suffices and you must find other things to consider. . . time to ponder the chasm between modern and ancient living.

Eating uncooked food has blessed me with gas and diarrhea rivaling an experience I sampled in Nepal. So I'm mellow, slow moving like a patient eighty-year-old yoga devotee. Time is irrelevant. Perfect plodding and rethinking the period from sun up to down.

As surely as cottonwood trees and animal tracks usually lead to water, my love handles have vanished and been replaced by skin stretched over my lower ribs.

My fire machine (bow drill) wouldn't behave. The ointment cap I used to clamp the top of the spindle burned through, and the spindle cut into the palm of my hand. Now I have no fire or cap for the ointment. Matted hair, scalp crusting, involuntary fast (the shits). My savage reawakened, I brave the hours either reapplying a body mud-sheen to repel bugs or figuring that's it high time for a bug snack.

A vision quest usually gives the questor a direction, a plan, a dictum, or a purpose for their life from that point on. The scope of this experience remains unclear, because I'm consumed by a few rudimentary issues, like suffering from ant-fly madness complicated by widespread body and scalp itchiness. Food fantasies wane behind a daydream of a hot shower that will sooth skull-dermis decay and cactus attacks.

Knocked out, I amuse myself by watching an ant war and wonder how the ages revolve, rockwise. Night birds conduct low flybys, a lizard bursts away on lightning-speed legs. But I'm too tired even to create indents in the sand that will prevent my hip and shoulder from falling asleep. Through a process of elimination (eating only sheep jerky), I link sheep jerky to diarrhea.

The group rejoins and is split in two, and we're on our own to travel thirty miles in two days without a guide. I'm heading into the river canyon with three other guys, and one of them begins stretching to prepare for exertion. I wonder: Do wild animals stretch before going for a run?

The common realization concluding survival schools is that you can do more with less. You also gain a renewed appreciation for modern convenience. Ancient cultures, and a few lingering native cultures, provide rites of passage that graduate their kinfolk into new levels of awareness. Getting your driver's license, getting laid after the prom, entering the military, or graduating college aside, Western culture fails to provide such signposts; getting in touch with the desert does.

Dyed red-orange after two weeks in Mother Earth's sandbox, on the final night I lull myself to sleep with thoughts of lizards and ants and anticipating bliss in the morning gas can of powdered limeade.

Reentry: A van ride back to Salt Lake City flirts with the present, but we still smell like cavemen. I woke at 4:00 A.M. in a Salt Lake friend's den, where it took me a minute to recognize that I wasn't in a really nice shelter. Sighting the first mirror, I winked, "Hey, *you* can survive in the wilderness." I was cutting a better self-image and still snacking like a fashion model — until I flew the next day to Scotland to sample a dif-

ferent sort of barley, the single-malt-scotch version. In flight, I began a voracious three-day food binge of triple servings, extra salt, and constant confection.

Flying back to a city, I looked out the plane window into a desert canyon and took a bit more home. And wondered if ants like sheep jerky.

"Do tadpoles contain protein?"

— survival school cohort, after
suckling water from a pothole

CANON 36: Pack a literary masterpiece.

While trekking among unclad Irian Jayan aboriginals I read this apropos inquiry in Henry David Thoreau's *Walden:* "It is an interesting question how far men would retain their relative rank if they were divested of their clothes."

"It is better to have a pigeon today than a peacock tomorrow."

— The Kama Sutra, read in a Karachi,
Pakistan slum while eating unidentifiable
slop in a fly-infested outdoor
food stall . . . on Christmas day

"The furniture of the hut was neither gorgeous nor much in the way."

— From *Roughing* It by Mark Twain,
read in an Argentine beach hut
featuring only a cot, clogged sink,
and porthole-window-supervised
sunbeam shining a trapezoid on the wall

CANON 37: What a difference a walk makes.

My dad and I were inspired to walk across Wales by our previous 225-mile, coast-to-coast stroll across Northern England from St. Bees on the Irish Sea to Robin Hood's Bay on the North Sea. Meandering twenty miles a day along towering shoreline cliffs, through dense forests, and over forbidding mountain ranges shaped our greatest father and son moments; and one benefit of undertaking an exhausting itinerary is that it left us no energy to recycle any debates about my tenth-grade car-crashing spree.

Hiking across the beautiful and changing landscape, we acquainted ourselves with villages forgotten by modern highways and high-speed trains, environments where heaven and earth appear to have been reversed. Our cicerone was the late Alfred Wainwright's map and guidebook. Wainwright,

known for his eccentric and solitary nature, became celebrated for linking the local footpaths, neighborhood shortcuts, and rural trails to fashion splendid, extended hikes.

A father and son roaming across rural England can be an inspiration for other lads and their dads. At seventy, my dad had endured a broken neck and two heart angioplasties. Despite the risks, we were off. As we rode our last train to the launch point, we sat across from each other. I watched him sleep; he looked lean and tired. What if he had a heart attack on a mountaintop? I was going to have to father *him*. Perhaps the kin tide of foresight and caring has now permanently shifted.

One of the keys to enjoying a coast-to-coast traverse is realizing that getting lost is half the fun. Occasionally we'd hike separately, one ahead of the other or on different routes. You understand a town when you walk in *and* out of it. Our feet held out without incident, hiking boots broken in before departure. I am told my English-born great-grandfather and his son walked the south coast of England together. Great-Granpa had some trouble with his feet and poured a bit of  whiskey into his boot "to make the leather more supple." Dad continues to scare the English with questions about wildflowers and the whereabouts of some carbonated Bass Ale.

globetrotter dogma

The traverse complete, we dipped our toes into the North Sea, victorious. We then returned to the aftermath of the Industrial Revolution. In the end, Dad slept less and ate more than I did and seemed to have more energy. He also noticed every birdsong, flower, shrub, and tree. Walking across rural England is a media sabbatical, a recess from a world seized by materialistic superstition.

Walking across a country is a more intense bonding experience than you'll find on any golf course.

The journey allowed me to rediscover the best friend I have. As we looked out over the North Sea, the conquered trail at our backs, my dad sighed, "Thanks Bruce, this has been a great victory in my life." A few thoughts came to mind:

"Nature will not be admired by proxy."

— Winston Churchill

"There's an adjustment period any time we change worlds."

— Barman regarding my warm beer

"It's an old dog for a hard road."

— Bed-and-breakfast hostess, Shap, England

CANON 38: "Objects at rest tend to stay at rest.
Objects in motion tend to
stay in motion." — Isaac Newton

Migratory behavior starts early. The first sign is typically sneaking out of the house while parents sleep. Migratory animals can't help themselves. There is no blueprint for this instinct that's as wired into our survival as hunger is. The urge to travel is like the impulse to laugh: You can't teach it, and you can't take it away.

"Every style that is not boring is good."   — Voltaire

"Chaplain set out to entertain and he created art. And the guys who set out to create art don't even entertain."
     — A. I. Diamond

CANON 39: You may not have it your way.

I winced when I caught my first glimpse of freshly lacquered, skinned, beheaded beagles and other dog torsos. More than one of my China dinners was botched when shallow buckets of dog and cat heads came into view. You soon realize that in certain parts of the mainland anything moving is edible. There seem to be colonies, or at least entire streets, dedicated to slaughtering and selling anything not human. You may find yourself sprinting to the end of one of these streets of carnage, deep in the throes of nausea. But that's only one facet of the country; China is wonderfully bizarre and beautiful too. Go.

"China is a big country, inhabited by many Chinese."
— Charles de Gaulle

"The odds are good but the goods are odd."
— Grizzly Annie on Alaska's disproportionately high male-to-female ratio

"Leisure is one of those evolving words that is redefined every generation or so."
— Pete Allen, tossing and turning in the middle of a mosquito-infested night sleeping on a picnic table in New Caledonia

CANON 40: Paddle upstream.

Imagine the perfect whitewater canoe odyssey, and you'll probably float through an unblemished, roadless wilderness on clear water with lots of rapids and riverside camping, where  the moonrise invites the tranquil call of the loon — just what I found whitewater canoeing Canada's Dumoine River.

My patient, wilderness-savvy helmsman pointed out that

+ toilet paper can survive anything when stored in a peanut butter jar.
+ canisters make handy outdoor spice containers.
+ plastic garbage bags, twisted within a sleeping bag sack, make great waterproof bags.
+ a bandanna around your neck minimizes the mosquito's pasture.

After some cajoling, he also let me in on the secret client-stereotype code:

Guide Wannabe: A know-it-all who might inquire, "Any job openings?" Also possibly a do-it-all.

Disappearing Act: Becomes invisible during camp setup/breakdown and during meal preparation. Comments,

"Hey, I turned over the canoes last night," as they show up on time for dinner.

Lily-Dipper: Low-energy paddler inclined to continually stop paddling to itch, talk, or look.

Bug Neurotic: Never stops talking about the bugs. Compelled to count and announce their number of bites (new and total). Incessant preventive actions including sprays, lotions, hooded bug suits (northern lingerie). Inevitably they get bitten the most. Also: nonstop itching and complaining. "Are the bugs worse than yesterday?"

Canoe Sinker: overpacker.

Other award-winning silly questions most commonly asked by clientele:

Is that a rock? (pointing at one)

How deep is it here? (while looking at the river bottom)

Have you seen the River Wild?

What do you do in winter? (Is river running all you do?)

What class is that one? (of every rapid and ripple)

Where do I put this? (fork, toilet paper, sleeping bag)

At what elevation do deer turn into elk?

Do we take out of the river at the same place we put in?

"I am the King of Rome, and above grammar."
— Sigismund, at the Council of Constance

CANON 41: Keep an eye on your dreams.

• • • **a**nd your ride home. A Swedish traveler landed in my Manhattan horse-drawn carriage back when the carriage business was still lawless. It was the final ride on the first night of my two-year driving career, though it nearly didn't last the night. The trusting Swede rode back with me to the stable area behind the sketchy western edge of Hell's Kitchen.

An equestrian rookie, I removed the horse's bit, since it seemed to be bothering him, before tying him off on a metal ring attached to the stable wall. Now the reins were attached to nothing. My passenger was seated in the carriage when the class-B racehorse spooked and bolted — still attached to the carriage — down Eleventh Avenue into oncoming traffic. I sprinted after the carriage, listening to the blare of horns, the skidding screeches of taxicabs, an hysterical foreigner, and the fading clop of hooves. The gap between the carriage and me widened to a block when the all-out galloper turned right onto one of the descending Lincoln Tunnel access ramps. A catastrophe seemed inevitable: a dead Swede, a dead horse, and the ultimate dishonor to my brother Bryan who trusted me to drive alone.

As the carriage disappeared into the tunnel, a man driving a pelted, muffler-free Chevy Nova slowed down to announce, "Don't worry, I'll get 'em," and sped off. I rounded the corner just in time to see the Nova skid to a halt just ahead of the barreling animal and cargo and the fearless stranger run to the center of the street and motion frankly for the horse to stop. When that failed, apparently bent on suicide, he stood directly in the horse's path until it nearly bowled him over. He grabbed the horse's head halter with both hands and, dragging his heels beneath the horse, gradually coaxed him to a halt.

I caught up, tried to breathe, fitted the bit back in the horse's mouth, and offered the hero the money in my pocket for saving lives and my job. "Nah," he replied, "I've done this before," and drove off, leaving me, my horse, and a speechless Scandinavian fifty gallops from the mouth of the Lincoln Tunnel.

"When the going gets weird, the weird turn pro."
— Raoul Duke

CANON 42: Keep it sweet.

Your parents may have honeymooned in Bermuda, and your DNA may have originated there too. The breezy, twenty-one-mile Fishhook Island consists of stretches of pink-speckled sand beaches separated by limestone cliff–rimmed coves. Churches and colorful stone and cedar architecture distinguish the undulating landscape, while convoys of white-collar tourist duos live out biker-couple fantasies, on mopeds.

Bermuda is more than a refined, secure haven for wealthy folks hiding money from governments and living off the interest. Local celebs include a *Guinness Book of World Records* kite flyer, Ms. Universe 1976, and Johnny Barnes — a seventy-ish, retired school bus driver who has dedicated his life to transferring smiles to everyone who transits around the island's busiest traffic roundabout. Every day from 5:00 to 10:00 A.M. Barnes *performs,* waving, smiling, gesturing, and preaching love to all. They've already dedicated a life-sized bronze statue in his honor just down the road from his roundabout. Soon after passing the real Johnny Barnes you encounter the iron version: Johnny frozen in his traffic-greeting glory, giving an evangelical salute, smiling, with arms extended above his

head. He apparently loves everything and doesn't keep it a secret.

When I asked him how to stay married forever, he replied, "Keep puttin' honey on it, to keep it sweet, or you'll be in trouble" (flashing a big smile). Barnes has been blissfully married since 1951.

Here in the midst of semitropical nowhere, an island never visited by war or fast-food franchises, the oldest British colony remains a fresh-air paradise for visitors, reinsurance corporations, wealth, moped pilot training, and one chipper, immortalized bus driver. Sweet.

"Sixty dollars, please."
— Bermudian cab driver, concluding a fifteen-minute ride

CANON 43: Don't haggle over nothing.

Avoid money hernias. Don't haggle people to extinction. Enjoy the sale. The same shoppers who bargain down an impoverished Javanese innkeeper fifty cents probably shop at the Sharper Image back home. The test of adventure greatness depends on the depth of the traveler's vision; secondary is their amount of time; and last is their bank account.

At home, don't become a sporting goods store conqueror. Do you really need a personalized odometer/altimeter for that day hike in Norway? Although K-Mart and Wal-Mart have crushed small-town intimacy, these retail-coliseums sell tents, hiking shorts, and other travel necessities priced far below the mall-rat outfitters.

"Finance Charge; current annual percentage rate: 21.740%"

— The fine print on a credit card statement

CANON 44: Concoct a mission.

The "I was really off the beaten path, they'd never seen white people before" rap is getting rather tired. Super, we're all Marco Polo. The best way to comprehend a culture and to harmonize with the locals is to devise a hobby-inspired crusade: birding, riding animal-powered vehicles, attending religious services, going festival hopping, tracking literary landmarks, learning a massage technique from the local healer, or watching musical instrument makers at work. Invent a quest, and find out where the local guru hangs out.

This strategy moves you past the bumbling tourists on deck to be fleeced by the bevy of con artists that plague many destinations. You'll save money by discovering the heart of the region's honest people.

"The big question is whether you are going to be able to say a hearty yes to your adventure."

— Joseph Campbell

CANON 45: Don't outlast your welcome.

Costa Rica's dense, musty jungle canopy recalls the hide-outs of our early ancestors. Alive with thirty-foot tree ferns, roaring howler monkeys, and a natural garden setting that beckons emerald toucans, the air is heavy with biomass musk. One day, enjoying the shade of moss, palms, and stringy vines and the constant bird chatter, I was interrupted by a spider monkey above. The territorial, beagle-sized monkey began a massive branch-shaking offensive. When I looked up, he gave me his best you'd-best-split-now glare, then delivered a targeted spray of urine drizzle. I moved on.

✦ ✦ ✦

In Kyoto, it was customary until recently for visitors to know that a serving of brown tea rather than green tea meant that it was time to leave.

"Hello, I must be going." — **Groucho Marx**

globetrotter dogma

CANON 46: Don't shake hands lefty.

In many parts of the world, latrine flushing and personal cleansing is done with the left hand using a few splashes of rainwater held in a nearby vessel inside of a very small room without a toilet bowl. Never offer your left hand to someone in such places.

Squatting low within a Goa, India, restroom (an outhouse accommodating a porcelain floor-level crater), I was frightened by a sudden slosh and clatter — odd, since traditional Asian toilets don't "flush" Western style. The commotion below, identified by peering between my legs, was caused by a spasmodic pink apparatus flapping about wildly. I exited, darted to the rear of the structure, and barreled into a humongous pig voraciously groveling its snout deep into the outflow pipe of the outhouse. These "pig toilets" are clever spin-offs of traditional Asian toilets, wherein you hunker down, resting your buttocks on your ankles, hovering above an opening in the floor.

What distinguishes a pig toilet from traditional undeveloped-country latrines is the ravenous pig that consumes your poop without delay. There's definitely a sensation of a closed-loop ecosystem when your waste is recycled back into the food chain before you've even pulled up your pants. (It grants a new perspective on pork too.)

bruce northam

"Keep moving."   — Hunter Thompson

CANON 47: Sing.

The mission loiters in Fiji. Efforts to establish Christianity in the Fiji Islands began in 1825 by the London missionary society, and were successful. For those who have sidestepped organized religion, their magnificent gospel singing is a reason to visit the ubiquitous Christian churches. I sat in on, and near, many of Fiji's five denominational churches, listening to soulful harmonies reminiscent of the deep American South. Methodist, Seventh-Day Adventist, and Catholic missionaries were especially busy here, building churches in nearly every settlement, motivating the stirring Fijian choir knack for a cappella soprano, alto, and tenor.

If not for the diving and snorkeling, come for the gospel music. If the Fijians treasure one thing they got from the missionaries most, it is music — sacred song — and they infuse it with magic, especially in the rural chapels. The church may be an unpainted building down a remote and rutted road, but through the doors and windows on a Sunday morn, curious and smiling eyes of children will beckon you in.

A village elder may read a psalm, and then the worshipers near the altar turn out to be a choir. With no musical instruments, these men and women lift untrained voices in glorious three-part harmony, praising the heavens with beauty few European cathedral choirs match. Their singing comes from the diaphragm and from the heart. Fijians' song is not modified for outsiders. The beauty of it is its passionate yet unaffected presentation — deep velvet from ages long past.

A gospel serenade lured me into Navai's Adventist Church, an agreeable, muggy Central Florida-ish, Kiwanis-style lodge, flanked on all sides by Venetian windows. After the children stopped sneaking peeks at me, they reset their attention on the preacher. Pacific Standard Time plus nineteen hours, and there was a message on the blackboard behind the preacher.

"God has a plan for you."

Below that, in reference to the "blessing line" of snacks available: "Banana Cake," "Stone Buns."

Swans sing before they die — 'twere no bad thing
Should certain persons die before they sing.

— Coleridge, on a bad singer

CANON 48: Make love, not war.

...hell, do both: get married! When you and your honey quarrel, chant the Chinese idiom, "Even a typhoon doesn't last a day." (Also reread Canon 18.) Quarrels often arise on departure and arrival days under the stress of laboring through airports and getting ripped off by unscrupulous cab drivers.

I piloted a horse-drawn carriage around midtown Manhattan for two years. Most of my passengers were couples. The most useful thing I learned from blissful older couples was that a sense of humor breeds timeless compatibility.

"But switching to a more interesting job usually means a pay cut."
— A couple arguing about posttravel employment

"Not everyone is wired for the unknown."
— Ex-girlfriend's mother

"Of all the things I've lost, I miss my mind the most."
— Anonymous second honeymooner

"The only victory over love is flight." — Napoleon

CANON 49: Give something back to the people through whose lives you pass.

Day after day, villagers see travelers tramp through their space, pay them for food, ogle their lives, then move on. Enrich the lives you pass through with a song, painting, sport lesson, donation to a local school or hospital, recipe, poem, grin, flowers, or an embrace. The possibilities are endless.

A doctor I befriended in India shared an inspiring story. It was the first week of life of a set of twins in a Bombay, India, hospital — each in their respective incubators — and one was not expected to live. A nurse fought against hospital rules and placed the babies in one incubator. When they were placed together, the healthier of the two threw an arm over her sister in an endearing embrace. The smaller baby's heart rate stabilized, and her temperature returned to normal. Embrace those you cherish.

In Bulgaria, giving flowers is an everyday tradition suiting any occasion. Always present them in odd numbers — even numbers are for funerals.

Live Loving
Die Dreaming

oitaph in a cemetery in Guayaquil, Ecuador

CANON 50: You only stumble when you're moving.

Speed walking through a maligned quarter of east England's port city Hull, I nearly tripped over a rhetorically blessed drifter, also thirtysomething, living in an urban lean-to, adrift in reverie. After a few canned lagers our conversation swayed to the contents of his tattered olive rucksack.

As he fished each item out, he surrendered histories of his worldly possessions and arranged them on the sidewalk, exhibiting and professing the import of rope, tarp, a risqué magazine, airline eyeshades, his "idea registry," and an antique army mess kit.

Last, he produced a damp, hulking dictionary, held it high, widened an eye, and swore, "Mate, *this* book's got everything."

"You have already arrived." — Thich Nhat Hanh

globetrotter dogma

CANON 51: Not getting what you want is sometimes good medicine.

If you're financially or occupationally challenged, celebrate the fat latitude of your freedom. We still have much to learn from our great American frugal forebear, Henry David Thoreau, a voice from the past that the world has been unable to ignore, even though it has barely listened. Thoreau lived happily in refined poverty near Walden Pond and warned us that our cure for the evils of complexity will likely be more complexity. He was convinced that struggling for most of the comforts and luxuries we consider essential costs us more than these things are worth.

We receive the signals and hear the calling but often ignore the royal thundering within, that voice asking what you truly need to be happy. Too many of us spend thousands shrinking our heads. *Out there* — on the edge of your own Walden — therapy is free. Wander. Let the woods be your church. Simplify. "Success" can limit as many options as failure; the workaholic lifestyle usually comes along with a pair of blinders that buffers us from other opportunities.

"No Gentle Ride, Man"
    — U-Haul "Gentle-Ride Van" revised with black tape at Burning Man festival, Black Rock City, Nevada

bruce northam

"I think that to get under the surface and really appreciate the beauty of any country one has to go there poor."
— Grace Moore

CANON 52: Remember.

In the midst of rambling coast-to-coast across Northern England, my father and I made our way up and down along Cleveland Way, a wide path that followed the ridgeline of a series of fells. On the summit of the highest mountaintop was the ultimate naturalist's epitaph for Alec Falconer, founder of the UK Ramblers walking club. A couchlike stone bench for two overlooked the lush, checkered farm plains of central England's North York Moors. There was a plaque set at foot-height, six feet in front of the seat at the base of the magnificent foreground view:

This plaque and seat were erected by his many friends in memory of

Alec Falconer
"Rambler"
1884–1968

Instead of staring at a tombstone, when you remember Alec Falconer you savor his divine outlook.

"What you're experiencing is basically a genetic echo — if you recline in cool moss early on, you want to lie down again." — Basil F. Northam

CANON 53: We hate nepotism, until it happens to us.

Tired of digging yourself out from beneath the workaholic rubble left behind by the Industrial Revolution? Even those marvelously skilled in handling the elements need a hand from time to time.

Experience is what every righteous traveler looks to acquire. In lovemaking it is equivalent to grace. Everybody wants it, but nobody seems to find it by traveling directly toward the destination. Unless born with experience or grace, nobody arrives there without sweat. If somebody lends you a hand, savor the moment, then pass that gratitude to someone else in need.

Thoreau suggested that we are rich in proportion to the number of things we can afford to leave alone.

"To humankind: The only animal that laughs, drinks when not thirsty, and makes love at all seasons of the year."

— a toast

CANON 54: Ask before you ingest.

The owners of the family-run paint store in Negotin, Yugoslavia, graciously took me in for the night and prepared a traditional Serbian dinner. One appetizer resembled oversized Chicken McNuggets. The interior of the crisped nuggets were off-white fine mush, a shiny, mangy tofu. "What's this?" I asked, ingesting my second sample. *"Pohovani mozak,"* came the answer.

The origin of this fatty-tasting, pungent paste was still not clear to me.

"Fried brain . . . cow," the daughter smiled. I tried masking my dry heave with a sneeze, and the snack exploded out my nose.

She corrected herself: "Cow and pig brain mix!"

✦ ✦ ✦

Inquiry: "This is *very* chewy; what is it?" — author, gnawing and miming laborious chewing

Response: "Woof" — Chinese restaurateur

CANON 55: Slow down.

Sometimes there is no payoff to rushing — the early bird only gets the freshest pesticides. Things take time; a study found that Mount Everest is moving steadily northeast at a rate of 2.4 inches a year because of the geological fault system that slowly pushes India under Nepal and China, creating the Himalayas.

The longest recorded flight of a chicken is thirteen seconds, so pushing the envelope can bring bad luck.

"REMEMBER YOUR LEVEL"   — Parking garage sign

"However vague they are, dreams have a way of concealing themselves and leave us no peace until they are translated into reality, like seeds germinating underground, sure to sprout in their search for the sunlight."

— Lin Yutang

CANON 56: Write a letter.

He was barely two years old, living on the rim of Managua, near Nicaragua's airport in a shanty slum resembling Bombay's most unfortunate neighborhoods. Walking down his dirt street, he carried a chicken that nearly outsized him. My thoughts transformed into an open letter and a few suggestions for a boy (and his country) about hanging onto things that really matter.

Dear Nicaragua Chicken Boy,

Knowledge is portable. In your case it was an official Republic of Nicaragua chicken. From afar, the daunting hodge-podge of corrugated steel and random billboards jointed into scrapbook housing looks inescapably dismal. Yet a random dirt-road stroll guided me to you, your enigmatic chicken, and a full cycle of emotions.

While you wait on domestic justice, chicken man, envision life from a juggler's perspective — maneuvering five airborne balls representing friends, kin, health, occupation, and your higher power. Keeping all these balls in the air becomes an overwhelming yet worthy chore. Understand that the occupation ball is made of rubber; if dropped it bounces back. The other four — friends, kin, health, and higher power — are crystal. If dropped, they are usually irreversibly damaged, never the same.

Vie for balance in your life, despite corrupt strangleholds on your national harmony. You live in a country where the dispar-ity between rich and poor accelerates. Embrace what is closest to your heart. Without passion, life pales.

After discovering you — Nicaragua's future — I retraced my inbound steps, leaving the neighborhood with one more thought for you and your contagious smile: Remember that earth-quakes and war have erased most of the physical relics of Nicaragua's cultural heritage. So talk to your grandparents . . . when they die, libraries burn. Carry that knowledge, amigo, and remain inimitable.

Your pal, Bruce

"What fuels our Gross National Happiness?"

— Anonymous

CANON 57: Put yourself in someone else's place.

While traveling, take the time to switch roles with the people you encounter. Imagine what it would be like to be in their shoes, meeting you.

Justice is never advanced by the taking of levity. Looking autonomy in the eye can be a true challenge, but after all, what effort could be too great in the praise of freedom? Your reasons are between you and your maker.

Seek companionship and mirth. There should be no cure for laughter epidemics.

"What we're seeing is a very significant crack in the health care system."

— Intellectual analysis of stingy corporate vacation allowances

QUESTIONER: *Are any of your plays about your own life?*
ARTHUR MILLER: *Not really, but I'm in all the plays.*

CANON 58: Exercise Halloween-at-age-twelve-style caution.

Be prudent. Monitor your partying. Many misadventures occur when we're under the influence. A buddy of mine and I were hitching across Australia when the two drunk creeps who'd picked us up suddenly veered off the main road onto a remote dirt byway. They got out of the car and pulled knives on us, demanding our money and packs, which were in the trunk. We were a flash away from being stabbed, and shock gave way to rage. We eluded puncture by clarifying that we were trained in martial arts and that no matter what transpired, one of the crooks would either lose an eye or have his throat disordered, even if they managed to stab us. Neither of us was trained in martial arts, but they threw our packs on the ground and sped off. That was back in the day when my pack was *everything*.

Ladies: There's safety in numbers. Women roving solo may want to band with a pack of locals or fellow travelers before roaming into the unknown. Hang out where the local women are. Heed no firsthand advice. Instead, get a second or third opinion.

Apply the Traveler's Safety Code of Conduct: It's okay not to trust everyone right away. Experienced travelers are not offended by cordial distrust between new acquaintances, even

if they share a room. It's accepted that life on the road makes one an easy target. If a friendship is being built to last, neither individual will take offense at precautionary wisdom — like toting your valuables with you every time you hit the toilet and storing valuables in your pillowcase while you sleep.

Unlike hit-and-run thieves, con artists have all week. Muggers and fighters typically have extensive experience in the field — hopefully more than you. Limit your losses. Give it away, run, or both. One must stoop to conquer.

"The major causes of problems are created by a drug interaction between alcohol and testosterone."
— Philosophical Venezuelan policeman

CANON 59: Dream out loud.

Imagine the process of choosing your sojourn as creating an image of the environment you want to explore and then organizing your energies into building it. This process necessitates being part dreamer, part builder. Innovation and growth result when you take risks and dare to experiment with your own life. Traveling doesn't always have to be unusual, however. In our alienated, fractured lives, we need an awareness of the sacred in the ordinary.

No guidebook can tell you how to choose your quest; at best it can catalyze and awaken the quest within you. You can paint by numbers and visit the tourist traps, but you'll never create a holiday masterpiece that way. A masterpiece demands the spirit and impulse of an artist. To construct the adventure of your life, you need more than travel agents and destination recommendations. You need to generate faith in your own trailblazing competence. Born in your heart, tempered by your mind, molded with your hands, and walked with your own two feet, the trail you blaze is your remarkable gift to yourself, everyone you leave at home, and whomever you encounter along the way.

Each new thing we learn creates new connections among brain cells. Regardless of age, an active brain produces new dendrites, which are connections between nerve cells that

allow cells to communicate with one another. Wisdom is built from a lifetime of memories.

Travel when you can; dream when you can't.

"Dreams take up a lot of space? — all you'll give them."
— William Least Heat Moon

CANON 60: Not all who bargain are poor.

Thrifty travel savvy extends your allowance and adds a memoir to your souvenir. Transactions should be win-win, not win-lose. Enjoy the sale. Bargaining is embarrassing only for fat cats who can't do cheap tricks.

So, spread your wealth . . .

Disperse valuables wisely while mobile. That way if you lose something — or someone loses it for you — you didn't part with your essentials in one swoop. Have a secret pocket sewn into your travel trousers and shirts to balance out the goods in your money belt — that thing that wraps around your waist, under your clothes.

The point is to minimize material injury in the event of loss. Don't carry it *all* with you unless you must.

P.S.: Regardless of whether you actually bring it home or not, always take your unwanted restaurant leftovers with you and give them to someone who may be begging for money.

"When money speaks the truth is silent."
— Russian Proverb

"Money is not required to buy one necessity of the soul."
— Thoreau

"If you would know the value of money, go and try to borrow some." — Benjaman Franklin

CANON 61: Don't let the flash blind you.

Beware of false advertising, the pole-to-pole fallout of globalization. Bait and switch is one of the oldest tricks in the book. In the United States alone there are more than two hundred species of firefly. Female fireflies flash to attract males and encourage breeding. Each species has a specific, patented signal. However, females can mimic other species' trademarked flash signal to lure a male and eat him!

Similarly, watch out for independent money changers who approach you in the street, offering an exchange rate superior to the bank's. Whether you engage them or not, a "police officer" bursts onto the scene — producing a fake ID — to fine both of you for the illegal transaction. The policeman demands to see your money — as evidence of the crime. Real police never ask to see your money. Scream for help, back away, or insist on calling the actual police.

Raise thy charlatan antennae — better now than thereupon.

"Its pure form is ideal for replenishing body fluid loss. It mixes perfectly with other drinks."

— Claim made on a jug of Malaysian water

"The road to enlightenment is strewn with many dinner salads."

— On the menu of an overpriced
San Francisco noodle restaurant

A Front got no back...
Foolishly Cool
hello being cool is good
and fine but just to
be you all the time
be cool can make you
blind or make you a
fool so don't be
crul just be you just
being your self and
nobody else. A front
is good but it don't
have no back then
it slack and I know
you don't want that

— P-Nut, a Charleston,
South Carolina,
custodian-poet

CANON 62: Be worldly.

Practiced epicureans dazzle with their wine and sushi discernment. Acquiring such sagacity usually necessitates study and cash. Even if you can't distinguish between sashimi and a tater tot, you can still jig with the connoisseurs — by plotting with waiters in advance.

When your party is seated, leave the table incognito and summon your server. Clarify that you will be ordering for the entire table as if you were born on a sushi ranch and that they should accept your incoherent blather (e.g., "wagahnowtinkoo") as holy writ. Request they take note, leave, and then dispatch a cavalcade of miscellaneous variety platters. Mollify any gray area by endorsing "exactly" with knowing head gestures. Combat any doubters by noting a new chef has just been flown in from northern Japan and that old standards here no longer apply.

As the waiter turns to go flabbergast the kitchen with your wondrous order, pepper in some English for the gang by reconfirming, "Fresh water and salt." Saki intake should diminish your need to further school the rookies.

globetrotter dogma

"A man who tells the truth is bound to be found out sooner or later."

— Adirondack logger trying to knock
the charm out of pomp

"The goal of the hero's journey is yourself, finding yourself."
— Joseph Campbell

CANON 63: Hop the fence.

Righteous things can happen when you wander into areas "not recommended for travel" by the State Department. My brother Bryan jumped on a random *jeepney* bus leaving Manila and ended up in a remote Northern Luzon village. He got lost hiking to a towering mountain summit as the sun set. Above the clouds, he had no food or shelter until he discovered a circle of native Filipino men who invited him to attend their dog-on-a-spit barbecue and keep warm. Not wanting to be rude, he said, "I'll just pick," but then ate a lot. They all slept curled up by the fire, occasionally waking to snack on another bowl of puppy with rice. "It was more fun than being kidnapped by Communists."

✦ ✦ ✦

Once, on a massive cruise ship, I unearthed the passenger-forbidden crew bar, a lawless zone where, if you encounter barroom disquiet, your case will be judged under Liberian law. (Liberia is Africa's floundering attempt at a slave repatriation country, and has one of the more corrupt governments on earth.) Registering cruise ships in Liberia is a bargain.

The underwater crew bar is a smoke-fogged, window-free, steel-hulled, army-baseish joint, a worker's hangout where the musicians, cooks, beauticians, maids, and Cartier peddlers mingle in thick smoke and 1950s Wisconsin beer prices. The crew makes up one-third of the three thousand people on board, and this is where they let their hair down. Only a portion of the international crew is allowed above deck into the guest zone. No guests are allowed down here. The trick was pretending to be one of the ship entertainers. This really is a no-no, so don't try it unless you can find a crew member to be your accomplice. For me, it was the only place to escape cruise-ship coma.

"People don't take trips — trips take people."
— **John Steinbeck**

globetrotter dogma

CANON 64: You are the source of all of
your relationships.

You can't give anything to anybody else that you haven't already given to yourself. Make a list of the values you seek in a relationship, such as respect, love, trust, awareness, sensitivity, intent, compassion, and thoughtfulness. List words you would use to describe an ideal relationship: wondrous, contemplative, hopeful, supportive, excited, anticipatory, emotional, lusty, optimistic, dreamy, humorous, honest, expressive, intense, forgiving, fantasizing. Then put the word *self* before each value and apply them to you. Clarify your assessment of what makes a relationship tick, then do that with yourself, a.k.a. self-bonding. Examples: self-respect, self-compassion . . .

The most important words in most languages start with the prefix *self*. English is limited in this respect, providing mostly negative associations like self-centered, self-sabotage, self-destructive, or self-concerned, as opposed to French, which is replete with positive associations with self.

Your relationship with yourself facilitates what happens out there. Whatever you are looking for in relationships, first establish those relationships with yourself.

P.S. There is only room for one delusional person per relationship.

"How do you know when you are following the right path?
Same way a kite knows."

— Robert Drake Martin, III

CANON 65: Sometimes you deserve the New Age Splurge.

I occasionally capsize my travel writing with headlong rollovers from jungle backpacking to Jacuzzis overlooking mountain-panoramic sunsets. My voyages into countries where you sup on the main course (rice) in candle-lit, bamboo-thatched huts gives way to hot lava stone massages in a $600-a-day New Age luxury resort — where white-jacketed waiter quartets solemnly present entrees of roast fennel, nopale cactus, corn and anasazi beans braised in saffron, anchovy chili, tomato broth with sea bass, gulf shrimp, mussels, and snow crab. I have to admit that this offbeat adventure bargain hunter sometimes finds it hard to put the backpack back on.

Tucson, Arizona's, Miraval health resort is where luxury and (some) physical exertion collide to mindfully navigate you "into the moment." I arrived at Miraval immediately following a three-week whitewater rafting excursion down the Grand Canyon section of the roaring Colorado River. Twenty-one days minus television and bathtub, I entered Miraval unaware that Clinton had been reelected and reeking of socks rotting within a muggy sleeping bag. This was Miraval's debut backpacker check-in.

It's Camp Comfort, affluence casually dressed. Cactus weather.

Following breakfast from a palatial buffet with place cards trumpeting the calories and fat grams of each portion, I was whisked away by van to the nearby horse farm and the first recommended activity of my stay, the Equine Experience — just as the dining hall's bird call–based New Age tunes were delivering me to nirvana. It was time to open a "door into the room of self-awareness and self-acceptance." Hmm.

The Equine Experience first introduces equestrian ground skills. A straightforward workshop for those perceiving it solely as an opportunity to groom a horse and then send your new pal galloping within the circumference of a pen. It's really a lesson in self-awareness: identifying and exploring your communication patterns that do and don't work, using one-ton horses who are amazingly deft at reading  humans. For instance, I tend to come on a bit strong sometimes and ignore the impact my approach has on people. But when the horse balked three feet sideways to escape my sudden semihyper gesturing, I noticed. As I calmed down, so did the

horse. I lapsed again when I tattled to the instructor, um, "equine facilitator," about a recent broken romance and sure enough, the horse froze up — another energy connection I never would have made on my own.

This brushing and combing session was certainly not my first experience with horses. I funded college by driving a horse-drawn carriage in Manhattan. I was kind to Jerome, my strawberry roan partner in the New York carriage business, and I'm sure we bonded, despite the fact that I didn't always "greet him first by gently touching his shoulder." My newfound perspective, however, made me aware of how sensitive horses are to human emotion (although I *did* know that Jerome enjoyed inhaling Big Macs in Times Square).

Then came the lesson on focus, Miraval style: hoof cleaning. My first attempts to lift and clean my horse's hoof bottoms were unsuccessful. He wouldn't budge. I couldn't figure out why. My facilitator correctly observed that I was thinking about ten things at once. She told me to stand back, focus only on the hoof, approach it with confidence, and pick it up. Yup. I stepped back, focused only on the hoof, and reapproached confidently. Hooves began lifting into the air.

Miraval's horses may be specially trained to empathize with humans. Unlike Manhattan carriage horses, they don't have to worry about subway steam spouting from potholes or snarling garbage truck dragons. Then again, neither do Miraval employees.

The final challenge was the liberty lunge, my bid to encourage the horse to walk, canter, and then gallop in a circle within a fence-enclosed pen. The whip in my hand (visual impact only), a reproving tone, and a march toward the rear of the horse convinced him to be off. To keep the show going I also sort of galloped in a circle within his. This circus trainer undertaking roused my inner cowboy. I stopped when we were dizzy.

"Horses will always take care of themselves," I was assured. "You only need take care of yourself."

One white foot – buy him;
Two white feet – try him;
Three white feet – look well about him;
Four white feet – go without him.

— Old English Rhyme

CANON 66: Wandering is a healing branch of medicine.

The tropical ring around the earth provides ample palmculture (palm-tree culture) alternatives for backpack nomads, divers, and package tourists. Fiji's largest island, Viti Levu, is dandy, once you rise above the crowds. In a small highland village I was invited by the village chief to take part in a *kava* ceremony.

The Fijians' delight in family life radiates. The friendliness of Fiji stems from tribal custom. Family and friends — old and new, often one and the same — are life's greatest gifts. Every child is taught four essential aspects of "chiefly behavior": respect, deference, attentiveness, and humility. A well-rounded person, say the Fijians, behaves as if everyone is of interest and importance.

I was greeted on the matted floor of the town meeting hall by the chief and his entourage for a customary *sevu sevu* greeting — similar to a Christian grace before a meal, except both host and visitor say quiet prayers, all heads bowed. Cool dusk set in. The rite commenced with a prayerlike communiqué and interpretation of my journalistic curiosity that segued into a *kava* drinking session — a chief's council bread breaking. *Kava* is the opiate of a substantial sector of Fiji's 850,000 inhabitants (well, most of the guys anyway). The *kava* bowl, the *tanoa*, is given an honored place. The *tanoa* is a block of wood with legs and a depression carved in the middle of it. Some bowls are more elaborate than others, with intricate carvings. Others merely serve the purpose of holding the beloved extract (I later celebrated with a bunch of guys in the airport, swigging from a big blue bucket).

Villagers sit cross-legged, shoes off, facing the chief. Primo *kava* is made from the long, dried root of a pepper plant *(Piper methysticum)* and water.

The murky grog was systematically distributed in a coconut half shell *(bilo)* around the semicircle of six seated men. The group ceremoniously claps *(cobo)* once — loudly, with hands cupped — to summon a person's six-ounce gulp, then acknowledges the quaff by clapping again three times. The grog tastes like faintly bitter, muddy Hudson River and eventually imparts a fine scotch-contemplative, euphoric grin. This tranquilizer first numbs your lips and tongue, then everything else. The buzz recalls a sort of earthy codeine canapé or a Native American mushroom blessing. The grin widens as the relaxation ritual endures.

The art of ceremony, a marvelous trance.

I downshifted. English-speaking, often literate, low-key Fijians speak in soft tones, switching between English and their native language, which reminded me of serene Italian. They remain calm even when exalting a subject of worship, like rugby.

These gatherings combine calling card, telegraph, telephone, television, newspaper, and gossip column, typifying community before electricity. Fijians begin drinking *kava* no earlier than sixteen years old. These are people who have preserved themselves secretly like members of a lodge who are not allowed to give away the secret of the handshake — a *kava* ritual unveils the secret. It was time to talk.

"You live in New York City?" the chief inquired.

"I do."

"Many people," he nodded.

"Too many," I agreed, then confessing that I often encounter a thousand people in a day, speaking to no one but myself.

That's when I think they prayed for me.

During a pee break, I reveled in the cool fog and full moon rising while two grinning children hid behind a colorful home, encouraging a game of hide-and-seek. To the south an isolated storm cloud steamed over a mountain, a communion of gray-white clouds flaring the high jungle sky with lightning and trailing drapes of rain.

My enchantment became official when an oratory attempt while snacking resulted in a spatter akin to implanting a banana into a fan. After a very sound sleep I woke on a matted floor, without a hint of a hangover, to the smell of breakfast being cooked by Mom.

Contentedness: what all the ages have struggled for.

"Every now and then we can be our Indian selves again . . . it's been programmed out, but it just doesn't die."
— Clammer Bob, a clam digger/sage in Beaufort,
North Carolina

CANON 67: Don't leave a trail.

Often, lightening your load becomes more trouble than it's worth. Unless you are certain that you plan to return to a place, don't subdivide and store part of your luggage with plans to pick it up "on the way back." Plans change. Lug everything, or permanently part with some of it. Tipping your cap to the shoreline for an indefinite period is the first step in discovering new lands. You may not want to retrace your steps, and carrying too much crap hurts your back.

✦ ✦ ✦

I trekked with a group of Nakota Indians across Saskatchewan, Canada. One morning, before going nomad again, we staged a "forest-debris-better-homes tour" to share our feelings about our self-made temporary homes built the previous night. In wilderness show-and-tell vogue, each builder stood before and critiqued their structure — makeshift twig, branch and leave huts that had served as last night's bedroom. The elder pointed out strong and weak points —

like an about-to-fall widowmaker tree dying above them. By the way, the only advantage to playing house on a sharp hillside is availing a running start from visiting beasts.

After discovering the designer animal in each one of us, we dismantled our abodes, like completed Indian sand paintings, scattered the evidence, and moved on. I'm struck by the impermanence of human beings compared to nature. This was such an important exercise in our expedition, but, then, we just dismantled them and moved on, leaving no visible trace.

"Rolling with only the destination in mind leaves the journey behind you." — Truck driver

"Follow pleasure, and then will pleasure flee,
Flee pleasure, and pleasure will follow thee."
— John Heywood

CANON 68: Kick the tires.

Before boarding any vehicle — especially buses and vans in countries where safety inspections don't exist — inspect the tires. Blowouts kill. Look for nails in the tread, worn sidewalls, bubbles, or other irregularities like light-colored cross-stitching anywhere. Alert the driver to anything suspect, and do not board. Likewise, always ascertain the driver's sobriety.

"Life is too short to be little."   — Benjamin Disraeli

The little Road says, Go;
The little House says, Stay;
And oh, it's bonny here at home,
But I must go away.

— Josephine P. Peabody

CANON 69: Practice people-watching.

Go incognito. A spare part of somebody else's conversation can make or break a dull day — and you might even learn something. If your life feels like an incurable sexually transmitted disease, look over at someone else. Eavesdropping isn't as risky as those ridiculous attempts at forced dialogue that typically backfire. It's okay if a tumbleweed rolls across the room (silence won't kill you). One of the first jobs of a traveler is to look unflinchingly at things.

Riding a Berlin train, the American notices that the German commuter with the wire-rim glasses — seated directly across — is staring at him without interruption. The stare continues. The American says hello, without warrant, to the dour onlooker, and the German dryly inquires, "Do I know you?"

Try these Casual Interloping Strategies:

1. Walking the dog
2. Wearing sunglasses
3. Using one-way mirrors
4. Toting a baby
5. Pretending to daydream
6. Pretending to daydream, nursed by cigarette smoking
7. Reading in the corner of a dimly lit café
8. Swinging on a swing set

Can you think of any others?

globetrotter dogma

"He that puts on a publick Gown must put off a private person."
— Thomas Fuller

"Self-plagiarism is style."
— Alfred Hitchcock

CANON 70: Stay the course, curse the stays.

The marshy mist hanging over home life clears when you leave for a while. Somewhere in your journey, make a checklist of things you want to accomplish and eliminate from the home front. Brain-dump everything and cross off items when they're either actualized or hurled into orbit.

Warning: Your Buddhist tranquility may diminish three weeks after returning home and you find your worldly self once again yelping at traffic jams.

It is Homo sapiens' nature to hesitate at the threshold of pathless woods. Just remember the ten most omnipotent words in our language: If it is to be, it is up to me. Ferret out your secret aspiration. In Hellenistic times, Plato declared public festivals as "breathing spells" concocted by the gods out of compassion for people's unyielding drudgery; the Greeks devoted half their year to hedonistic pursuits. So should you. Go do your thing.

We travel not to elude reality, but to prevent reality from eluding us.

"May you enter Heaven late." — **Kemmerlin Book**

CANON 71: There will be moments when you don't know if you can visit a certain place. There will be a lifetime of knowing that you did.

In 1922, my grandfather, James O'Sullivan, a captain in the fight for Ireland's independence, emigrated from Ireland to the United States via Canada — one year after the partition of Ireland and simultaneously with the death of his associate Michael Collins. He traveled west, laying Canadian rails, cowboy ranched in Montana, then hitchhiked to Manhattan's Upper West Side, where he opened and ran the popular O'Sullivan's Chophouse — in a neighborhood of Irish bars — for thirty-five years. Shortly after establishing himself in New York, his wife-to-be also emigrated from Ireland.

With that in mind, Mom and I visited Eire in tribute to her parents — and to see if the Irish would reciprocate the hitch-hiking hospitality James O'Sullivan enjoyed in 1925 America.

In this land of fiercely independent people who value their

poets as highly as their warriors, our strategy was to be road-warrior day-trippers and elegant country inn evening guests — upscale vagabonds. At first, she waved at cars to request rides, but the drivers only waved back. We needed a hitching sign, so I crafted four cardboard appeals: Mom, Angel, Innocent, and Pub, which worked best at small town intersections.

"So Mom, where should we venture today?"

"Never ruin a hike with a reason," she winked.

At that moment a car — piloted by an eighty-five-year-old woman — pulled over. We rode on narrow, stone-walled roads past thatched cottages, castles, fortresses, churches,  and other noble dwellings. A prime-time radio talk show host mused about gardens and the comings and goings of birds in the yard: "In the last fifty years it's been fashionable to sneer at tuberous begonias" . . . "Magpie birdhouse raids scaring off other birds" . . . "The tits will come along quickly." Real world news. Then a "lost pet alert" followed by a stolen bicycle appeal. Mom reports, "Dad won't put out bird seed. He thinks it's welfare." The rain comes again. Our driver acknowledges, "The rain is fond of Ireland."

The landscape changed to sheer cliffs, wet meadows, rocky moonscapes, and roofless abbeys. We pass a damp, lush, lime-colored farm teeming with cattle. Pointing to cows, Mother chimes in with "mootopia!"

This enchanted Atlantic island foray reminded me of my mother's many traits — unconditional love, kindness, safety — and introduced me to others: She snores like a house on fire!

We were in for a shock — we are dropped off at a pub, even though we were picked up using the "Angel" sign. We ease into the social glue of pub life with a Guinness. Mom sits closer to the band playing music by the fireplace. Foot tapping gives way to knee slapping; soon she is dancing.

Then it dawned on me — the sign I forgot to make for her, representing what my mom stands for: Love.

"Wherever they may in the distance roam, this country is never forgotten by its born."

> — Barman, looking over at my mother
> doing the Irish jig to live pub music

"Hugs remind us of who we are."   — Mom

CANON 72: Contemplate.

Highland Irian Jayan Melanesian aboriginals live in tidy, wood-thatched, grass-domed huts called *honays*. Men and women sleep and pass time in separate two-story huts. I was permitted to sleep, and reflect, in *honays* after receiving consent from a village chief. Certain bungalows are the privilege of men who've established themselves as warriors. A tad rustic if you focus on the fleas and mice, these alpha-male sanctuaries are fertile pastures for the imagination — all around hang shrunken animal heads, spears, weaponry, and charms.

These aboriginal men converse in very soft tones, if they speak at all. There we sat in a circle, puffing clove cigarettes and noshing on soft, warm sweet potatoes enveloped in dimly lit smoke, illuminated only by a well-tended fire. A serene Cannabis euphoria was obtained by inhaling tobacco as deeply as the rest of the guys. Knee-deep in nomadic cache, I accepted the silence as meditation, in a corner of the world where safety pins were once fair trade for a shrunken human head.

"The spirit of a country is like a wild animal. The more you chase it, the more it moves away. But sometimes — if you're lucky, if you sit quietly in one place and wait — it will come to you." — Andrew Bill

CANON 73: Don't frighten thyself.

My wilderness survival course in the southern Utah desert included three days completely alone. In a red canyon so beautiful it makes other parts of the earth lonely, after two weeks in Mother Earth's sandbox, I am dyed red-orange. My senses are alive. I smell the sage breeze, hear the wisp of darting vultures, see the dry earth crackling under my feet, feel the precious seconds ticking.

This desert, like most, can experience sixty-degree day-night temperature swings. This chilly night in this sandstone-cactus backcountry, I tried lulling myself to sleep with thoughts of an all-you-can-eat buffet. Simulating sleep, burrowed deep inside my burrito-fashioned poncho, hat pulled down completely over my face, listening to my breath, when a large-footed animal, possibly a human linebacker, encroached. The sound of legs brushing against brush started and stopped abruptly. My adrenaline flooded as it drew close. It stood above me; I lay stone-still. The steps became more erratic as my heart raced. I froze, waiting for the intruder to decide my fate. It just stood there. I blinked. It stepped. Blink. Step. The sound of my heart thudding against my eardrums overtook all clamor. I held my breath, then realized that the nervous commotion was indeed my eyelashes moving against the inside of my hat.

The next morning, I stood up and assumed the unshaven, hunter-gatherer stance. My inner savage reawakened, I had a few questions: Is engaging in a relentless verbal solo while alone weird? How come *abbreviated* is such a long word? Why do we say something is out of whack? What is a whack?

"We need the tonic of wildness."   — Thoreau

CANON 74: The rat race will still be on when you return.

Guaranteed. Besides, the problem with the rat race is that even if you win, you're *still* a rat.

Why is it that Americans are granted about one-third the vacation time of our European and Australian allies? Four to six weeks of paid holiday is standard, and often the law, in most of Europe. Swedes can receive up to two months of freedom per year. From days past, the Hopi Indians took off

half the year, the Ashanti of Ghana skipped work for 200 days a year, and Kung Bushmen preserved 230 days per annum for soul searching. Only the Japanese, with an average of one week off per year, are on a clearer path to self-destruction.

The key reason for the disparity is that Americans have fewer workers' rights. It's unlikely that a government legislature will transform our holiday legacy in this particular plane of existence, so get busy rocking your own dream dinghy. Corporate downsizing, temporary employee agreements, dwindling benefits, and merciless economics should not limit your opportunity to visit assorted societies.

"A little rebellion, now and then, is a good thing."
— **Thomas Jefferson**

CANON 75: "Every taboo is holy." — Eskimo saying

Toll the bells for indulgence. Well-behaved people seldom make history. Being a provocative rascal may result in a considerably shortened life . . . but what a way to go. Traveling is mightier than you — it does with you what it wishes. You won't change fate by rushing into it. Best to wait, leisurely, for it to overtake you, preferably in the company of friends. I've never seen a hearse pulling a U-Haul.

On India's Anjuna Beach I participated in a full-moon dance party thrown by the resident Western hippy nomads who are still busy elbowing the edge of the psychedelic frontier. These untamed, clothing-optional cotillions rage till dawn, the campfire amplifying the Day-Glo face paint. Undulating to the electronic music *sensurround*, expatriate moms grooved lavishly to the rhythms while simultaneously breast-feeding their babies. Talk about lactose tolerance.

Life is a situation comedy that will never be canceled; we are put in the material world to get more material.

At the same time, remember the possible negative effect your regalement may have on the local populations.

"Don't let the bastards bump you from your orbit."
— Anonymous

"I used to be snow white, but I drifted." — Mae West

"Something that chases and catches things."
— Native Alaskan Yupik translation for the word *man*

CANON 76: Contemplate Incan law.

The pragmatic rules governing Incan society are rekindled by visiting Ecuador's Inga Pirca, the northernmost outpost of the Inca Trail, constructed by the *Cañaris'* in 1150 and modified by the Incas until 1527. Established atop a 10,500-foot mountain, the campus is an aggregated religious temple, military fortress, political outpost, and solar calendar for figuring seasons for planting. From outer space the construction resembles a puma.

The Incan Code dictates: Don't lie, don't steal, don't be lazy. The penalty for murder requires undertaking your victim's workload for life — in addition to your own occupational obligations.

"O.J. did it." — Ecuadorian bus driver

globetrotter dogma

Find a role model. Learn from the existing traveler subculture. How do I get started on the Southeast Asia trail? Partner with a grizzled road warrior who dropped by three years ago and hasn't left.

One line from the poetry of departures: The trip starts before you leave. Befriend a fellow globetrotter at the airport, before the plane boards. The alert ones, wearing sensible footwear, next to the luggage without wheels — and imparting the impression that they wouldn't be crushed by a rainstorm — are easy to spot.

Ask questions. One enduring world traveler I know supports his crusades by piloting a horse-drawn carriage around Manhattan's Central Park (which is how I got to try it for two years). He has lived out of backpacks for twenty-five years and rarely parks for longer than a season.

When you put this guy on paper, color drains like a dying trout — to steal a few excerpts is like trying to define sibling rivalry in a sentence.

Roaming is his life.

Nonetheless, I wrote down my interview with this wanderer:

Do you miss being young? A child can turn an empty lot into a jungle, a droopy tree into a forest, or a bedsheet into a Sunday-morning fort. If snow fell, you packed it; when leaves

fell you picked colored ones. I remember an attraction to mud, avoiding concrete unless at school, and balancing on anything that looked like it needed it. Climbing along the length of a rusty golf course fence became hiking a Himalayan knife ridge. I still think and live this way.

Reflect on a surreal experience. Warm organs hauled from a deer's chest diced with coriander and garlic. It's bad manners to refuse wedding food from a Lisu hilltribe family in Northern Thailand.

How is one seized by wanderlust? Curiosity and the attention span of a common housefly led me onto America's highways hitching in the 1970s when trust prevailed. A cardboard PLEASE sign helped, and hiking fifteen hundred miles on the Appalachian Trail really flipped back my blinders.

Are you in touch with nature? Humans are part of nature. I'm a street anthropologist who believes that we all fit into different tribes, but drifting is tolerated. There you are in Burma's outback . . . you feel heat on your neck, the tribe sends a scout to check out the backpacker — it's raining, and they know it.

Nature touched me once . . . hopping freight trains, I ended up in Jasper, Canada. Slept on the edge of town with a beer buzz, forgot to hang my pack. Rustling in high grass, an oncoming black bear ignored my territorial yelps. As I lay frozen, he sniffed my sleeping bag and then nudged me from head to toe. He tore apart my pack, wolfed my Kool-Aid and a loaf of French bread, then wobbled on.

How do "politics" affect world travel? Lightning bug sparks have caused prairie fires, bad breath has killed cactus, and politicians really do care. Currencies, like moods, inflate and deflate.

How does a carriage driver hold someone's attention? Remember you're competing with TV. A pond without an inlet or an outlet stagnates. Cut to the chase.

Why is TV so popular? You can't have sex all the time.

What does adventure mean to you? My dad instilled in me a keen sense of escapading. A teacher with a romantic imagination and plenty of vacation time, he loved setting out on aimless quests. Long ago, he coined a term: booming — intuitive, blind adventure — commonly on dirt roads that disappear into deer trails.

And your mom? Mother Teresa in plain clothes.

What's the downside of a nomadic lifestyle? A stimulus junkie always wants more — higher peaks, more primitive tribes, and one more off-limits, spooky nightspot. *That's* when it's time for another ten-day silent meditation retreat or a drive down to Central America.

"My Peter Pan never left, and we still hang out."
— The Wanderer

CANON 78: "Everything must end; meanwhile
we must amuse ourselves." — Voltaire

Seize the exhilaration of roaming. Let yourself in on the following secret: Life is short, so have fun while you can. Make a difference and reach out to people where they live. Go see for yourself — your goodness reflected in the image of others.

Long ago in the United States, probably during the Industrial Revolution, the vocation gurus forgot to pencil in sufficient time off for their workforce — a hapless plan. The consequences prevent most of us from exploring the secluded fringes of our planet. Nevertheless, you can afford to sidestep the prescribed decorum of amassing gadgetry that ultimately narrows your chances of ever venturing into remote cultures. First of all, the following common but irrational traps need to be sidestepped:

1. Fear of losing ground in your career
2. Hesitancy about blazing your own expedition trail
3. Inability to get some distance from your workaday life to clearly recognize what you do and do not value

123

4. Reluctance to ease back on the lawnmower throttle
5. Blind allegiance to the American lifestyles portrayed by fabric-softener commercials

"We are all responsible for our own happiness."
— Fijian coconut farmer

CANON 79: Get wild. You can recreate anywhere.

The defining highlight of an otherwise dull New York Yankee baseball game I attended materialized in the eighth inning when an animated fan escaped from the out-field bleachers and ran onto the field, disrupting the game. The game transformed into applauding the nimble, sprinting daredevil as he eluded three stocky security guards for five minutes — tag extraordinaire. An adult version of elementary school keep-away brought the packed stadium to its feet. With each failed attempt by the security guards to dive and capture the ballpark fugitive, the fans redoubled their grand-slam-style uproar. When the fugitive was apprehended, the security guards were emphatically booed. Just before the hero was hauled out of sight and pitched into the stadium penitentiary, he managed to wrestle one arm free and wave his cap to the crowd — a victory gesture that earned him a

final, frenzied ovation. People just don't have to be grown up all the time.

"Travel writers fear boredom more than death."
— Travel writer

"Gonna break my rusty cage and run."
— Johnny Cash covering a Soundgarden song

CANON 80: Just say know.

Drugs are dangerous. Don't do them. And if a drug requires you to regurgitate before it takes effect, take particular care. Prowling Taiwan in 1987, my travel partner Pete and I encountered a fellow American who manufactured spare Harley Davidson parts in Taipei (sorry to share that news with devout made-in-the-USA Harley fans). In search of adventure, our expatriate guide suggested that we consume three tablets of an over-the-counter "medication" called Romular that was formulated for people with special "psychological endowments" and promised heightened awareness.

The recommended dose was two tablets. The opportunity was assessed and detonated. After the obligatory vomiting, we visited an open-air rooftop disco. The world began to pulse and spin, and the hallucinogenic quaalude invited us to dance. My mind said talk, my body said *slinky*. After a dozen attempted encounters with innocent patrons, I noticed that my query, "Can you tell I'm on drugs," wasn't helping. I glued myself to a barstool next to the guys who'd already forsaken socializing.

Later, when we were gawking in the streets, the fish market street vendors couldn't figure out why, after painstakingly inspecting their entire inventory, we didn't make a purchase. I swore the fish were still alive and recognizing life around them.

Upon arriving home at dawn, our guest house gatekeeper surveyed our blank-stare grins and soiled clothing (playfully deranged, I had decided to crawl across the discotheque dance floor), then waved us through, asking, "Come back from where?"

"When everyone thinks the same, nobody thinks."
— Unknown

CANON 81: The real measure of your wealth is how much you'd be worth if you lost all your money.

Individuals plugged into good fortune glow in any light, whether it be from a ballroom chandelier or the bulb illuminating the janitor's closet.

Money is sometimes the way that people without talent or imagination keep score. One benefit of being broke is discovering who your real friends are. Plus, money is not edible and sartorial elegance doesn't have much pull in New Guinea.

Another bright side to lacking funds is increasing your vulnerability, since you can't afford to insulate yourself in upscale hotels or on private transport. This type of travel leaves you open to consistent reaffirmations of hospitality that are natural in most human exchanges — reinstating the grace that typifies random interaction. Being vulnerable makes it easy to intersect with luck.

I don't know why it is that the people who peek over the hill each month at their unpayable bills are invariably more entertaining than the folks juggling fat investments.

Poverty can be genteel, perhaps. This equation seems also to exist in drinking establishments in the form of a beer price–fun inversion: As beer prices decrease, rollicking increases. Conclusion: Stress kills, or at least gives you a stomachache.

"No shame in being poor. Abraham Lincoln was poor."
— **Filibustering Manhattan street-corner metaphysician**

CANON 82: We are not alone.

If we shrunk the earth's population to a community of one hundred people and kept all the existing human ratios, there'd be:

57 Asians
21 Europeans
14 from the Western Hemisphere, both north and south
 8 Africans

52 females
48 males

70 nonwhites
30 Caucasians

70 non-Christians
30 Christians

89 heterosexuals
11 homosexuals
 6 people possessing 59 percent of the entire world's
    wealth, all from the United States
80 living in substandard housing
70 unable to read
50 suffering from malnutrition
 1 near death and 1 near birth
 1 (yes, only 1) with a college education
 1 owning a computer
    and 1 lucky bastard on the road, meeting all of the
    above . . .

Viewing our home in these terms, our obligations to understand, welcome, and educate are clear.

"Every man dies, not every man lives."

— William Wallace

globetrotter dogma

CANON 83: Don't repeat…unless a place beckons.

Some days the curtain rises on a reluctant bed exit and persists with a woebegone commute, unsavory work chores, and no glimpse of foliage. This day, on Fiji's Taveuni Island, debuted with a jungle trek from coast to coast, crossing the island's mountainous center ridge. The route, beginning in Delaivuna, periodically broke into lush green fields of wild horses munching beneath teeming, sixty-foot palms.

I also encountered snakes and a few frontier families living in autonomous homesteads. These stopovers doubled as water fill stops from roof-rainwater tanks that crown many Fijian homes. Villages typically have communal tanks.

Descending to within earshot of the ocean, a footpath led me through another lush garden, past a banyan tree with a one-hundred-foot perimeter sprawl, emerging into Navakawau and the field in the midst of twenty homes for a round of communal Frisbee. Dozens of naked three-year-olds assemble and

scatter according to disc bearing, while older onlookers try their hand at giving plastic flight. Dripping with sweat I was led to a small beach beneath draping palms and was encouraged to engage in

one hour of tossing-forty-kids-into-the-water, repeatedly. Laughter echoed for miles.

I was led by the kids to another waterstop, then further uphill to rejoin my trail. As I was ascending through a bright green garden of tarot, cassava, and papaya plants, a sunshower cooled the air...like walking in heaven.

Rejoining the trail back to my campsite, I felt fatigue setting in when I encountered a man in his sixties who was standing in the middle of the path, clutching a machete. At first I thought he glanced at me in a fairly conspiratorial way — asking if I needed anything from the market back in town. Realizing that I never consulted with the chief before entering this village, I guardedly reasoned that I didn't need any supplies. Silence. Though famished, I was simply too exhausted to backtrack.

Eroni Tabua, eldest son of Navakawau's chief, then asked if I'd like to have lunch. Again, I explained that if I was to make it back to camp by dusk I needed to move on. He then insisted that we take a five-minute detour off the trail. I followed the machete man into the thicket, slightly paranoid.

Eroni stopped and shook a few trees and plants, caught a few falling objects with one hand, and began craftily machete-hacking me up a very timely fresh coconut, copra, and papaya variety plate. He tossed each fruit into the air a few times, whacking it rapidly with knife in mid air, catching the slices and handing them to me.

His family owned the plantation where I had dined. There in the heart of it, Eroni's soft-spoken voice carried the kindness torch for the world, as pleasant and intelligent as any thoughtful professor of the humanities.

I opened my Fijian phrase book to derive another word for thanks. Instead, the kind farmer took the book, opened it and randomly found a word, *pikiniki*. Definition: picnic!

Having such a character machete hack a fruit plate while you stand in the midst of his plantation discussing tarot farming explains some things, like peace. Before I walked on, Eroni contemplated my inevitable return to Fiji and said, "Next time, come home straight away."

✦ ✦ ✦

What is travel? Earth localized.

"Hitch your wagon to a star." — Ralph Waldo Emerson

"Departure should be sudden." — Benjamin Disraeli

"The foxes have holes, and the birds of the air have nests; but the Son of Man hath no where to lay his head."
— Matthew 8:20

CANON 84: The good old days are now.

The destination is not ruined. Ignore travel snobbery. Bali, Thailand, and other supposedly overrun paradises are still great places to visit, even though they may have been more "real" fifteen years ago. 'Tis a haughty condescension to insist that because a place has changed or lost its innocence that it's not worth visiting; change *requalifies* a destination. Your first time is your first time; virgin turf simply is. The moment you commit to a trip, there begins the search for adventure. Intrigue will find you.

The grass is always greener on the other side, especially when you first arrive.

"Very beautiful . . . many factories."
> — Jeong Lyle Lee's reply to my question,
> "Is Kwangju [Korea] beautiful,
> or are there many factories there?"

"Imitation cannot go beyond its model."
> — Ralph Waldo Emerson

CANON 85: Don't talk politics.

• • • Or religion, unless you are very good at it. For example, you're gathered beneath a palm leaf–thatched Thai restaurant pontificating with two Germans, an Aussie, a Swede, and a Brit when the state-of-world political discussion surfaces. They all pick on the American. Take the fifth, or try this one: "Smaller countries have bigger outlooks."

Adages like "avoid talking about religion and politics" float because such banter sinks — especially with new acquaintances. Such topics are usually the recycling of someone else's third-hand propaganda. Try steering conversations inspired by newspeak toward music, hobbies, and relationships — editorials in which individuals are truly experts in their opinions.

You get to know somebody faster when they speak from the heart. Engage people in conversations about topics that are dear to them and not hotbeds of contention influenced by the media. People enjoy talking about their hobbies and the things they know best.

Here's one example of an innocuous political commentary: The only smiling currency portrait is Ben Franklin, because he was never president.

"It's not my fault."

> — Canadian traveler defending herself
> against the misfortune of a small
> Indonesian village — just wired for
> television — that was glued to a
> "professional" wrestling match

CANON 86: Get back into the kitchen.

The kitchen is the most fun room in the house, the world over. Deep in the heart of Morocco's Riff Mountains, I hiked a rocky hillside shadowed by olive trees. I befriended a thirty-year-old shepherd wearing a ski cap crowned by a pom-pom. He was the commander of fifty goats and twenty sheep.

After a lesson on flock-control fundamentals — tree branch coaxing, pebble throwing, grunting, and hissing — we exchanged butter rum Lifesavers and cashews. I helped bring the herd home to his dwelling, lost somewhere in the narrow, winding byways of Chefchaouen. Moroccan sunsets are forever on my mind.

We settled in the dirt-floor kitchen, drank some sweet Moroccan mint tea,

and smoked *kif* (tobaccoish, pipey-smelling stuff) from a sixty-inch *Sebsi* pipe. The peace pipe ceremony gained momentum when his mother, brother, and sister arrived and we all played the Arabic-English name-that-kitchen-utensil game. Meanwhile, in the next room, the livestock *baaed, grunted,* and *mooed.*

+ + +

Even if you're not invited into the kitchen, it is sometimes necessary while traveling in distant lands to supervise the chef. A way to discover and monitor what's happening to your food is to get invited into the kitchen while they prepare your meal. When language barriers are insurmountable, point at the items you want and see for yourself that meat or other portions are fully cooked. Bring home the recipe.

"Ladies and gentlemen, this is your dining car attendant. I had the baked chicken, and it changed my life."
— **Amtrak employee announcement**

CANON 87: Track your mentor.

Stalking Wolf was raised free of reservations in the mountains of northern Mexico. Born in the 1870s during a time of great warfare and violence, he was part of a band of Lipan Apache that never surrendered. He was taught the traditional ways of his people and excelled as a healer and a scout. At twenty, he began a sixty-three-year wander throughout the Americas, seeking teachers, learning the old ways of many native peoples, and never participating in modern society. At eighty-three he encountered young Tom Brown, who became the recipient of Stalking Wolf's personal wisdom and hundreds of years of Apache cultural insight. Brown learned these ancient skills as a child (and adolescent) in New Jersey's Pine Barrens. Highly attuned to nature, the scouts were part of a secret society who refined tracking, awareness, and wilderness survival to an intense science and art form.

Today, Tom Brown's Tracker School teaches survival basics: finding shelter, water, fire, and food. You're taught to build a debris hut, start a matchless fire using a self-carved bow drill (imagine fiddling a bark ribbon bow across an upright paper towel holder to spark an ember), make cordage by reverse wrapping long grasses into strong string, build dead-fall hunting traps, track animals or humans by analyzing their print "pressure release," and enhance your natural awareness using wide-angle vision. There are workshops on selecting edible plants, hunting with a throwing stick, and stalking — or meditating — by way of "fox walking."

Attendees graduate (at least) as versatile Neanderthals with a reactivated primitive sensibility, discovering uses for a knife beyond buttering. The mentally demanding curriculum unearths parts of your wild side and is not for anyone rendered miserable by camping in the rain, confronting poison ivy, or eating stew ladled out of a ten-gallon steel pot.

The Apache scouts were the masters of the wilderness. Most modern folk are aliens in the wilderness, and our ability to survive within it equals the ultimate freedom. Brown has elevated tracking to an intense science and art form. When I spotted a paw print, he certified "a disk-fissure crest-crumble lobular pressure release." Translation: "a strolling female fox with a full stomach who paused here and looked left." On one field trip, Brown led us along a forested trail. Within a fifty-yard segment of the trail he wrote on ice cream sticks to identify fifty different tracks (left, right, or rear print) at the otherwise invisible tracks of ten different animals. Brown doesn't miss a beat in the woods.

Brown's passion for the Native American way of living in commune with nature and a loathing for environmental destruction burns in him, making the Tracker faculty more than a fraternity of nomads who like sneaking up on animals.

What if your plane crashes and you are left alone, freezing

naked in the woods? Consider refining your outdoor survival skills, and the Native American philosophy of connecting with the earth.

"When somebody moves something in your house, you notice it. When somebody moves something in the woods, I notice it." — Tom Brown, Jr.

"Inspector of snowstorms."
— Henry David Thoreau's self-appointed title

CANON 88: Take note.

Archiving is a timeless delight. If your computer doesn't come along with you (Mark Twain, John Steinbeck, and Karen Blixen seemed to manage without one) a sturdy, pocket-sized, inconspicuous journal can be your best friend. I use the dual-lobe format: Front to middle is the chronological journey (left brain accounting), back to middle registers miscellaneous inspiration, addresses, to-do lists, and other nontrip-related deliberation (right brain musing). When they meet midway, it's time for a new ledger.

Journals larger than passports are easily lost and alert others of your reporting.

To protect against documentation loss — travelers who lose *everything* on the road ultimately only regret losing their film and journal — photocopy and mail home or transfer your musings into cybercafé emails to yourself and friends. Alternately, the emails you send can be perfect journal entries. Later, your physical journal is an enduring backup in case of computed meltdown.

Also, simply claiming to be writing a story permits enthused questioning and poses no threat of idea bankruptcy.

If your travels don't keep you up at night, your report won't keep anyone else up either. The story you tell is the life you live.

"Be a good date."

— Kurt Vonnegut Jr., lecturing on writing

"I put a piece of paper under my pillow and when I could not sleep I wrote in the dark." — Henry David Thoreau

"Be careful in traffic. Mopeds are often the family cars in many Asian cities. Taipei, Taiwan, has wide, busy streets that seem to have no rules. Lawlessness, such as ignoring signals, is aggravated by leaning on the horn. Single-stroke fuel emissions cloud the air. It's common to see up to four people crammed onto one scooter. They move freight as well. Today I saw a fellow weaving through traffic on a small scooter while hauling a king-size mattress and box spring on his back."

— Author's journal entry

CANON 89: On the other side of fear is freedom.

Hardship reminds us of this truth, as does divine intervention. Driving across Ireland with a friend, Erica, we met a Limerick bartender-savant who wore a patient, empathetic expression. We sat down before Jimmy O'Sullivan's large bar-cum-lectern, and topics swung to relationships when Erica divulged her current crisis. Jimmy listened solemnly to her love-gone-bad tale, then began, "Young lady, allow me to explain how I ended up in the advice business. I spent twenty years as a death and dying counselor, where I reached out to terminally ill people and their families facing their worst moments. Repeatedly, I was reminded of how it usually isn't until people court death that they realize what a pity it is to not identify your passions and migrate toward them fearlessly. They'd all wonder — what did I have to lose? — just as their curtain lowered on what truly matters and what is meaningless. After twenty years of dealing with people who finally got clear on what they thought they were meant to do with their lives when it was too late, I committed the rest of *my* life to helping vibrant people like yourself to realize their dreams."

Erica began to blurt out a sentence but was interrupted.

"If I were to give you a million dollars right now, what would you do with it?"

After a breathless pause Erica responded, "I'd use a third to build a secluded mountain home, another third I'd invest wisely, then I'd travel the world until the rest evaporated."

Jimmy invited Erica to expound on those plans. Five minutes of her fantasy had elapsed when he asked, "Is the boyfriend in that picture right now?" A perplexed look stole onto her face, she swallowed hard, shook her head, and whispered a solemn no.

O'Sullivan peered at her from beneath a lowered, white eyebrow, "Contemplate who is and who is not in your dreams."

They should hand out plaques for that sort of therapy.

bruce northam

"The wise man travels to discover himself."
— James Russel Lowell

"A smile loosens stiff hearts, melts angry icebergs."
— Basil F. Northam

CANON 90: Assume an identity.

Fabricate an ID. Bogus journalist IDs, student cards, or business cards stating you are anything you aspire to be are easily procured in Bangkok, Hong Kong, Amsterdam, New York, and other lawless metropolises. I've wielded my "journalist ID" to slip into untold concerts, Knicks games, and MTV award parties. Shhh . . .

If you are budgeting (that is, camping or sleeping in hostels or dumps), enjoy the bathroom and poolside chaise lounge at the fancy hotel or resort across town. Bring a quick-change stash in your daypack. Act familiar.

Understand the rules so you know how to break them shrewdly, and mum's the word. Or simply redefine yourself as a *voluptuary:* one devoted to sensual pleasures.

"Commando crashing, sir."
　　　— Brad Olsen's response to a Winnipeg, Canada,
　　　　police inquest about our city park campsite

"I've got a damaged moral compass."
　　— Roger Yespy, reasoning with a resort security guard

CANON 91: Carry a phrase book and dictionary.

Because I lacked a dictionary, my sanity fuse was tested on a third-class train ride across China when there was "no room" in the sleeper car. It was my third sleepless night. There were scores of snoozing Chinese families on the floor and in the spaces between cars and nowhere to stretch out.

Flocks of chickens ran up and down the aisle, a caged piglet moaned beneath my seat, and lumbering sides of butchered meat covered in flies swung  from the overhead luggage racks. Mothers periodically poised their babies outside the windows of the moving train so they could poop. Black diesel engine smoke blew into the car, which never went faster than forty miles an hour. All the while,

vendors paced back and forth, endlessly peddling peculiar dried crustacean snacks. One group, snacking on a greasy chicken carcass, seemed to amuse themselves by drooling profusely and orally expelling any undesirable foodstuffs about the car. Not a napkin in sight. Coughing up and spitting phlegm onto the floor was also part of the drill. If I'd had a dictionary, I could have asked the right question sooner. I finally comprehended that an eighty-cent payoff was required when the conductor held up a banknote and made the "shhhh" gesture. He then led me into a totally empty sleeper car for my nap.

"When a man has something to say he must try to say it as clearly as possible, and when he has nothing to say it is better for him to keep quiet."

— Leo Tolstoy

CANON 92: Judge not.

People are usually more complex than initial impressions convey. Frequently, upon meeting someone, our debut inquiry is, "What do you do?" for "what you do" is often misconstrued as who you are.

A virtuous, nomadic man lived in consumer exile for decades before transforming into a famous spiritual leader. Evolving as a teacher, he chose a wandering, impoverished lifestyle to comprehend suffering and need. In his travels, the still unacknowledged sage wearing paupers' clothing requested shelter at the home of a mogul and was rebuffed.

Forty moons later, the sage, now a motivator of the masses, returned to the mogul's town. This time his presence was met with great fanfare, and he arrived in a splendid limousine. The mogul contacted the sage at his hotel to offer the hospitality of his home. The sage then instructed his driver to drive to the mogul's home. When the mogul rushed out from his home to greet the sage, he found an empty limo. He called to ask, "Why did you send over an empty limo?"

The sage replied, "I sent you what you really wanted. Some years ago I came to your house, and you scorned me. Now you wish to have me. I reflected — I'm the same man I was then — what has changed today? What do I have now that I then lacked? A limo. Apparently, that's what you really wanted."

Sometimes money is how people without talent or imagination keep score.

"The moment the slave resolves that he will no longer be a slave, his fetters fall. He frees himself and shows the way to others. Freedom and slavery are mental states."
— Mahatma Gandhi

CANON 93: Follow the surfers.

If you are bargain hunting for fun in the sun, trust that the career surfers have touched down where Valhalla has no service charge.

. . . but don't follow me into the subway. When I was twenty-one I lived in Queens, New York. One night at 3 A.M. I was returning home from an indulgent Manhattan debutante ball. Waiting on the station platform, sporting a tuxedo, overwhelmed by impatience, and inspired by a robust champagne buzz, I jumped onto the subway tracks and ran beneath the East River all the way to Queens in the surreal tunnel. I eluded passing trains by pinning myself against the dank tunnel wall. Upon arriving at my station (Queensboro Plaza), I climbed up onto the platform, straightened my collar, and nodded to the crowd waiting there for the next train.

Getting there is half the fun . . . but don't try this at home.

"Most people have that fantasy of catching the train that whistles in the night." — **Willie Nelson**

CANON 94: When minds shift, feet lift.

People handle adversity in different ways. To generalize, some crumble, some prevail. I met a coastal North Carolina café manager in a gas station. Months before our encounter, a disease threatened her eyesight until risky surgery extended her vision indefinitely. This crossroad redoubled her sense of seizing the moment. She was now attempting to drive to the doctor's office for a postsurgery checkup —

a visit that would reveal whether her vision would be extended or diminished — when clouded vision forced her to pull over.

I drove my new friend to the doctor's office and joined her in the waiting room. The chemical used to dilate her pupils made her uncomfortable, and she closed her eyes and leaned her head on my

shoulder. To me she felt battered but not beaten. I also sat in on the exam. The doctor looked through the ophthalmologist examination machine into her eyes while she gazed, blankly, hopefully forward with her chin perched on a level. Waiting for instant news on either darkness or light. Hopeful tension, then the relieving news that the occasional cloudy vision spells were par for the course. Six more months of sight were promised. Joy flows into her soul, an angel reli(e)ved. . . .

I rode back into her town to visit her café — where she resumed working the morning shift, pouring coffee for a team of old sailors and fishermen along the counter, shining light into all of them. I got the sense that she freely nurtured many otherwise lonely souls, never anticipating reciprocation.

She had the will and the *why*... and at least six more months to enjoy it with her own eyes. Every ending is a new beginning.

"I think about all the different ways we leave people in this world. Cheerily waving goodbye to some at airports, knowing we'll never see each other again. Leaving others on the side of the road, hoping that we will."

— Amy Tan

"Live, girls. . . . Live!"

> — A feminist optimist misinterpreting
> an exotic dance lounge sign

"It matters not how long we live, but how."

> — Philip James Bailey

CANON 95: "Not all who wander are lost."
— J.R.R. Tolkien

There is a bizarrely inefficient and wholly lunar border crossing linking Bulgaria's northwest corner to Serbian Yugoslavia. Almost exclusively used by foot traffic, the no-man's-land kilometer between immigration guardposts has the appeal of a concentration camp. I walked quickly past the lookout towers and barbwire. Midway was a horde of gypsies, indefinitely delayed in their attempt to enter Yugoslavia — and likewise kept from easily reentering Bulgaria.

At first, their quietude signaled another encounter with the refugees of failed Communism. One of the men stood up and summoned me, his teeth looking like a picket fence in disrepair. Attempting to enter a country recently bombed — far and wide — by NATO, I was a bit on edge.

"Come from England?" he suggested.

I told them I was American, and they all took a second look at me. The frontman looked back at the crowd, had two conversations, and turned back to me.

"Why you go fast?"

I jokingly looked at my wrist (where people usually wear watches), tapped it repeatedly, and mimed that I was in a rush. He stepped into the crowd and reemerged carrying a pogo stick and set it before me, inviting me to jump on it. I snapped out of my traveler's trance and sprang into action to discover that this was exactly what I needed to do that day.

I bounced around for a while, once springing into the laughing crowd — who were now clapping to the beat of my landings. Repurposed, I handed the pogo stick back to the mayor. All around were grins and other timeless symbols of content, uncomplicated by geography.

Destinies meet each other from time to time. Fortune comes to those who smile.

"No connections and only ourselves to recommend us."
— Rendering of gypsy interpretation
of immigration scrutiny

CANON 96: "Fall down seven times and get up eight." — Buddhist maxim

I f trouble finds you, don't surrender the lesson connected to it. Unsettling things happen. Move on.

Disgruntled by a flight delay in the Philippines, my brother instantly changed heart when he chanced on an impoverished seven-year-old boy wearing soiled rags who was joyously flying a kite he constructed by tying a long string to a billowing plastic trash bag. Why worry? Sometimes the well-to-do tend to dwell more on luxury problems than on real ones.

My other brother's reality was challenged further. While he was skinny-dipping on an African beach, keeping his pack and clothes in view, a merciless thief stole it all and sprinted into the jungle before he could swim ashore. He paused, naked and knee-deep in surf, sans money, passport, and clothes. Talk about starting over. The sympathetic villagers eventually restored his material basics, and the process of reestablishing his identity drove him deeper into the community fabric than any *dressed* person could have ventured. We become blindly enslaved by our possessions, and to be without

can be a blessing. The adventure begins when the plan is foiled.

"No trip in the fun, no fun in the trip."

— Wandering sage

"We're thinking your luggage might be in Nebraska."
— Greyhound baggage attendant, New York City

"Look up! As the stargazers say, beauty is only a light switch away." — Anonymous stargazer

CANON 97: Budget.

Freedom isn't always free. Travel should submerge you in wildness, not debt. Sometimes a budget (money divided by plan, or vice versa) is like the rudder on huge oil tankers, a necessary evil: A good one will get you there with style and ease, a bad one will probably get you where you're going eventually but will leave a mess behind. And without a budget, you may not go anywhere — at least not anywhere fun.

Spontaneity *is* a traveler virtue that, when destitute, can take on a limp.

globetrotter dogma

If you're not bursting at the seams with cash and still long for balance, remember this: Freedom of time is liberty of self.

"No money, no honey."   — Las Vegas apostle

CANON 98: Post art.

So you want to write? Aspiring travel writers might dare sending editors nifty postcards from the road. Write theirs only after you've practiced penning about the panorama to your pals. Muse about stamp options and use two or more of the coolest ones you can find. Stamps on the back of one of your best photos are as original as they come (or go). And remember, the pencil is mightier than the pen; mistakes are erasable.

Dear Landlord:
I always get homesick.
The closer to
home I get, the sicker I get.
Love, Tenant in 3G

Landlord

"I would hurl words into the darkness and wait for an echo. If an echo sounded, no matter how faintly, I would send other words to tell, to march, to fight."

— Richard Wright

CANON 99: Find someone to spoon with.

esson: Sleeping outside in light clothing without a blanket
or sleeping bag on cold desert sand sucks, even if you're in
a fetal clutch with limbs tucked inside shirt. Without advise-
ment, in the middle of the night, our wilderness survival guide
pointed to a hillside announcing, "Go sleep." Shiver dreams
became shiver reality. My sunrise anticipation prayers
included reciting the Doors' chant, "Waiting for the sun."

I woke by rolling into a turgid cactus and bit out the thorns
in my foot. I was already becoming an animal. The group
assembled for a solemn morning meeting. The two guys sporting North Face jackets didn't sleep at all; my hooded "Princess
Cruises" windbreaker, though failing to reaffirm my manli-
ness, fared better. Since most body heat escapes into cold
ground, a brief, after-the-fact lecture on the criticality of creating a puffy brush mattress was useless
even to those of us already knowing
this; the previous night a few dug
futilely into thorny nests, gave up,
and collapsed from exhaustion.

The guide also mentioned
that, at night, cold air settles
downhill like water, so one must
seek slightly higher ground when

hunting shelter. That and spooning with someone combines and redoubles body heat. None of the guys looked at each other.

After another freezing night spent jogging in place to warm up between naps, the next morning a few of the guys came together realizing that it was time to rely on one another and beat the cold by sleeping within spooning range. Outback lessons of survival won out over ego.

"All I'm trying to do is not join my ancestral spirits just yet."
— Joshua Nkomo

CANON 100: Travel is neither an art nor a science, but a notion.

And notions can border on logic, literally border logic. Stretching the value of a Rail Europe pass can encourage racing longer distances — usually overnight when you can't see anything — between major cities. Flying between capitals, especially in different countries, links urbanity, not sanity, and misses the midway magic.

Strategy: Take the train to a small town near the border of your next country, spend the night there, explore the place, and get the lowdown on bus, taxi, boat, or foot traffic into the next country — an adventure in itself that inevitably helps you

merge with locals. Likewise, enjoy the fringe of the new country while hunting the nearest train station — and continue the journey.

This way you sense the change transpiring between domains, explore untouristed terrain, and save money (a one-way ticket from Belgrade to Budapest, for example, costs eight times what two individual tickets purchased in Yugoslavia and Hungary would cost — and traverses nearly the same distance). Of course, you are on your own crossing the border.

Down to Gehenna or up to the throne,
He travels the fastest who travels alone.

— Rudyard Kipling

CANON 101: Ride, but pull over. *(Yes, bonus canons.)*

To worry is like rocking in a rocking chair. It gives you something to do, but gets you nowhere. So why worry that my Japanese motorcycle mysteriously died on an alien, stenchy range of Brooklyn's Belt Parkway?

A shirtless, resolutely tattooed Harley Davidson lowrider with a Kaiser helmet pulled over. His pipes resounded, about as loud as the ones that frenzy every car alarm along Ninth Avenue while simply idling at red lights. He killed the engine and walked slowly back toward me. Pulling down his sunglasses, he stood looking vaguely upset at my Honda Shadow. Our eyes met after an uncomfortable moment, where he peered at my bike, eyebrow lowering and rising. An unspoken, general feeling of mistake hung in the air. Then he walked back toward his bike, restarted, revved the engine, and burned rubber ten feet forward. Stepping off his bike again, he halfturned to find a rope in the saddlebag, tied it to the rear of his bike and the front of mine, and voiced, "Brake when I brake."

He towed me, snaking through crawling traffic, to a Honda dealer five miles away. Tow time was beautifully weird, like a carnival ride, being motorcaded by the lawless bellwether of a new sense government. At the garage, he untied my bike and said, "Next time, don't buy a rice burner," and rolled away.

An aging face told that his life agreed with him. Glad is a place: Motorcycling. If there is a better release, more wind, freer imagination, then you must be falling from a plane.

"Be who you are and say what you feel 'cause people who mind don't matter and people who matter don't mind."
— Dr. Seuss

CANON 102: Take a media sabbatical.

If you haven't circled the globe yet, maybe there's an umbilical cord attached to your TV convincing you that the world is an unfriendly place. *It's not.* The "news" is 95 percent hyped, manipulated ghoul. You *can* do it.

Close your eyes and imagine that you are eighty-five years old, rocking away, contemplating your life. How would you feel if you'd never had a genuinely wild journey? Globetrotting isn't for everyone, but here you are — questioning what lies beyond this prodigious land of mountain ranges, shopping malls, plains, baseball stadiums, coastlines, drive-through restaurants, forests, lakes, and 37 percent taxation. If you can't stand the thought of not taking a big trip, start packing.

Of course, there is a lighter side to the US News. From the West Yellowstone, Wyoming, newspaper police report:

+ A woman reported loud music coming from a neighbor's house.
+ A woman from the Grizzly RV Park reported that people were parking in a space she had paid for. She

had asked the people to move; they refused and had become angry.

+ A man reported that while the Coca-Cola man was delivering at the school someone deeply scratched the word *sucks* into the paint.

+ A man reported someone was duck hunting too close to his house.

+ An officer was flagged down by an individual stating that four juveniles were running around the Crows Nest Hotel knocking on room doors and creating a disturbance.

"No shoes, no news, no blues."

— Burmese "resort" motto

CANON 103: The mind grows where the mind goes.

Travel seeds tolerance. Roving introduces us to ourselves. Vacation is I; travel is we. Vacations hardly scratch the surface, whereas traveling — living there — opens the door into people.

"A stranger's eyes see the clearest."   — Charles Reade

bruce northam

"Leisure is the mother of philosophy." — Thomas Hobbes

"When you go to an inn let it not be with the feeling that you must have whatever you ask for." — Confucius

"I'm not saying yes, I'm not saying no. All I'm saying is maybe."

— Dad's response to repetitive childhood interrogation by me and my brothers on many long family car trips

CANON 104: Action is the antidote to despair.

It's time to reinvent NOMADness on earth. Nomadic behavior nurtures world peace: a planet where I no mad at you, you no mad at me. Don't get even, get odd. Stagnant people rarely make history.

I was in Berlin the week before September 11 terrorist attacks on the Twin Towers and the Pentagon and came upon an underground omen — small, neatly scripted graffiti, barely decipherable in the dusky crimson glow of an underground nuclear fallout shelter beneath the city: "He who shoots first, dies second."

Outfitted with its own air and water purification systems, an unintentional safeguard against panic in this fallout shelter — while in use — would be the availability of only 50 percent of our typical oxygen intake that would tranquilize the maximum capacity of 3,500 people into a slumber.

When I stepped into the shelter's in-house morgue, I joined an elderly English woman who was staring into a corner, deep in thought. After two moments (hers and mine), she whispered that she'd lost her home to a Second World War bomb. Silence expanded. Then she guaranteed that in any war, truth is the first casualty.

"I have seen that life persists in the midst of destruction; therefore, there must be a higher law than that of destruction." — **Mahatma Gandhi**

EPILOGUE

Can a wise man read another man's future?

In 1987 I was backpacking in the newly "opened" China when Chen entered my life. He was a multilingual restaurateur and the unofficial mayor of Yangzhou. He had a kindly way with backpackers, and one afternoon he invited me to join him on a seventy-mile journey in his rickety truck across southeast China's surreal limestone landscape.

En route, we passed a seemingly ancient man and his goat who were walking on the roadside in the opposite direction. Barefoot, the man plodded along the rough, hot road, two immense bags of rice suspended on a long pole across his back.

We passed him without a word, but returning to Yangzhou several hours later, we found him again — still plodding along. I suggested to Chen that we offer him a lift. We pulled over. The old man and Chen had a brief exchange. Then Chen got back behind the wheel, and we drove off, leaving the man in the road. Puzzled, I asked Chen to translate their conversation. Chen explained that the man wasn't due to arrive in Yangzhou until the following day. If he

were to show up in advance, he wouldn't know what to do with the extra time.

"You see, my friend," Chen smiled knowingly. "Not all of us are in a hurry."

I asked him to turn back. I wanted to ask the old man a few things. Chen parked, and I hopped out. The old man stopped, balancing on his walking stick, and grinned. We pondered each other, beings from distant corners of the planet — different planets really — worlds and ways apart.

Chen translated my questions.

"What's the most important thing in your life?" I asked.

The old man looked to his left, made a strange honking call for his goat, but did not reply. Was the goat the most important thing? When the animal arrived at his side, the man looked at Chen and spoke slowly.

Chen translated, "He said that if you can't help people, don't harm them."

I asked, "Why are people hurtful?"

I didn't look at Chen as he spoke, but rather stared into this old man's eyes. He was human art, more serene than a sleeping cat.

"If you decline to accept someone's abuse, then it still belongs to them," he said.

"Why do we quarrel?" I asked.

"The rise of a man's mind from his scrotum to his skull can be a long haul." We all burst into laughter.

The goat bleated. Chen said, "Ready?"

The old man and I shook hands and waved good-bye. The truck rolled away.

Today, I often recall the man's deeply wrinkled face, and I know that the infuriating fixtures of modern life — traffic jams, rude people, the arrogance of ego — are only *options*. His words remain a permanent, benevolent echo.

I departed Yangzhou a month later. Chen walked with me to the bus stop. After a hearty embrace, I told him how much his friendship meant to me, and that the old man's words were unforgettable. I thanked him for that too.

"Use those words to end a book," Chen said.

"Come on, Chen," I replied. "Do you know how old I'll be by the time I get published?"

"The same age you'll be if you don't," he winked.

Well, fifteen years, twenty letters, and four books later, I received a birthday card from Chen. I was in for a shock. He confessed that he hadn't actually translated the old man's words. Everything I'd learned had actually been Chen's sage advice.

"Freedom arrives when it occurs to you."
— Johanna O'Sullivan

"How difficult to imagine this place without a human presence; how necessary."
— Edward Abbey

bruce northam

ACKNOWLEDGMENTS

To everyone affected by the events of September 11, 2001 — keep traveling. It reconfirms that good outshines bad . . . every time.

Thanks to:

My *big* brothers, Basil and Bryan.

The kin and comrades who unblinkingly support my nomadic inclinations.

Libraries around the world, for letting me set up shop every now and then. Honorable mention: Beaufort, North Carolina's public library.

The Adirondack mountain pine trees — living in buckets and coffee cans — that enliven my Manhattan apartment.

My agent, Frank Weimann, and the Literary Group.

Katherine Dieter for introducing me to New World Library.

Jason Gardner — the editor of this book — for his talent and composure in handling a jigsaw-puzzle manuscript.

And a tip of my cap to Jorma Kaukonen and Joe Satriani, whose guitars free my mind and keep the lamps trimmed and burning.

bruce northam

ABOUT THE AUTHOR

Bruce Northam is the author of *The Frugal Globetrotter* and *In Search of Adventure: A Wild Travel Anthology.* His multimedia presentations — held at universities and seminar centers nationwide — celebrate the spirit and soul of circling the globe five times, freestyle. Bruce is Writer at Large for *Blue Magazine,* a guest writer for *National Geographic Traveler, Details,* and the *Utne Reader,* as well as a guest speaker on National Public Radio's *The Savvy Traveler.* His rambling résumé includes acting as a stunt man in Chinese action movies, judging Nicaragua's Corn Island beauty contest, surviving on sheep jerky in the Utah desert, dirty dancing in Venezuela, and babysitting in rural Japan.

Bruce keeps one tentacle in Manhattan. He is currently creating his next book and television show — both titled *American Detour.* Details on his live travel presentation are on **AmericanDetour.com**.

NEW WORLD LIBRARY
publishes books and other forms of
communication that inspire and challenge us
to improve the quality of our lives and our world.

For a catalog of our books, audio,
and video programs contact:

New World Library
14 Pamaron Way
Novato, CA 94949

Telephone: (415) 884-2100
Fax: (415) 884-2199
Toll free: (800) 972-6657
Catalog requests: ext. 50
Ordering: ext. 52

Email: escort@nwlib.com
Website: www.newworldlibrary.com